Published by MJF Books
Fine Communications
322 Eighth Avenue
New York, NY 10001

100 Things You're Not Supposed to Know
LC Control Number 2006933072
ISBN-13: 978-1-56731-849-4
ISBN-10: 1-56731-849-5

Copyright © 2003, 2004 Russ Kick

Originally published in two volumes under the titles *50 Things You're Not Supposed to Know* and *50 Things You're Not Supposed to Know, Vol. 2*. This edition is published by MJF Books in arrangement with The Disinformation Company Ltd.

Disinformation is a registered trademark of The Disinformation Company Ltd.

Original design and layout by Rebecca Meek. Adapted by Lisa Chovnick.

Printed in Singapore.

MJF Books and the MJF colophon are trademarks of Fine Creative Media, Inc.

TWP   10   9   8   7   6

100 THINGS YOU'RE NOT SUPPOSED TO KNOW

RUSS KICK

MJF BOOKS • NEW YORK

CONTENTS

CONTENTS

CONTENTS

CONTENTS

What turns a fact into something "you're not supposed to know"? Basically, it happens when that piece of information is upsetting, embarrassing, discomforting, or even damaging to a powerful party. The list of such parties is long — leaders of nations, legislatures, militaries, intelligence agencies, justice systems, regulatory agencies, corporations, mainstream media, the medical establishment, the educational system, religious institutions, racial and gender groups, academics and scholars in various disciplines, guardians of public morality, followers of ideologies, hypersenstitive leftists, conformist rightists, and others.

Other resistance comes from the fact that every historical figure has developed a cult of worshippers and cheerleaders who utterly refuse — in the face of all evidence — to admit the failings, hypocrisies, and, in some cases, the outright fraudulence of their idol.

In other cases, a fact doesn't offend an easily pinpointable institution or group. Instead, it's taboo because it exposes societal lies, the fables we tell ourselves in order to sugarcoat harsh reality.

With this in mind, it's time to present a cavalcade of troublesome facts, compressed and boiled down to their very essences so that you can quickly digest them in an info-glutted world. For further explorations, references are given in the back. ☼

Acknowledgments

Thanks to Anne, my parents, Ruthanne, Jennifer, Billy Dale, Brett & Cristy, Darrell, Terry & Rebekah, Mike, Matt, Gary, Richard, Alex, Rebecca, Jason, Disinfo, and others who've slipped my overstuffed mind at the moment.

01
THE TEN COMMANDMENTS WE ALWAYS SEE AREN'T THE TEN COMMANDMENTS

First Amendment battles continue to rage across the US over the posting of the Ten Commandments in public places — courthouses, schools, parks, and pretty much anywhere else you can imagine. Christians argue that they're a part of our Western heritage that should be displayed as ubiquitously as traffic signs. Congressman Bob Barr hilariously suggested that the Columbine massacre wouldn't have happened if the Ten Commandments (also called the Decalogue) had been posted in the high school, and some government officials have directly, purposely disobeyed court rulings against the display of these ten directives supposedly handed down from on high.

Too bad they're all talking about the wrong rules.

Every Decalogue you see — from the 5,000-pound granite behemoth inside the Alabama State Judicial Building to the little wallet-cards sold at Christian bookstores — is bogus. Simply reading the Bible will prove this. Getting out your King James version, turn to Exodus 20:2-17. You'll see the familiar list of rules about having no other gods, honoring your parents, not killing or coveting, and so on. At this point, though, Moses is just repeating to the people what God told him on Mount Si'nai. These are not written down in any form.

Later, Moses goes back to the Mount, where God gives him two "tables of stone" with rules written on them (Exodus 31:18). But when Moses comes down the mountain lugging his load, he sees the people worshipping a statue of a calf, causing him to throw a tantrum and smash the tablets on the ground (Exodus 32:19).

In neither of these cases does the Bible refer to "commandments." In the first instance, they are "words" which "God spake," while the tablets contain "testimony." It is only when Moses goes back for new tablets that we see the phrase "ten commandments" (Exodus 34:28). In an interesting turn of events, the commandments on these tablets are significantly different than the ten rules Moses recited for the people, meaning that either Moses' memory is faulty or God changed his mind.

Thus, without further ado, we present to you the *real* "Ten Commandments" as handed down by the LORD unto Moses (and plainly listed in Exodus 34:13-28). We eagerly await all the new Decalogues, which will undoubtedly contain this correct version:

I. Thou shalt worship no other god.

II. Thou shalt make thee no molten gods.

III. The feast of unleavened bread thou shalt keep.

IV. Six days thou shalt work, but on the seventh day thou shalt rest.

V. Thou shalt observe the feast of weeks, of the firstfruits of wheat harvest, and the feast of ingathering at the year's end.

VI. Thrice in the year shall all your men children appear before the Lord God.

VII. Thou shalt not offer the blood of my sacrifice with leaven.

VIII. Neither shall the sacrifice of the feast of the passover be left unto the morning.

IX. The first of the firstfruits of thy land thou shalt bring unto the house of the LORD thy God.

X. Thou shalt not seethe a kid [ie, a young goat] in his mother's milk.

◻

02
ONE OF THE POPES WROTE AN EROTIC BOOK

Before he was Pope Pius II, Aeneas Sylvius Piccolomini was a poet, scholar, diplomat, and rakehell. And an author. In fact, he wrote a bestseller. People in fifteenth-century Europe couldn't get enough of his Latin novella *Historia de duobus amantibus*. An article in a scholarly publication on literature claims that *Historia* "was undoubtedly one of the most read stories of the whole Renaissance." The Oxford edition gives a Cliff Notes version of the storyline: "*The Goodli History* tells of the illicit love of Euralius, a high official in the retinue of the [German] Emperor Sigismund, and Lucres, a married lady from Siena [Italy]."

It was probably written in 1444, but the earliest known printing is from Antwerp in 1488. By the turn of the century, 37 editions had been published. Somewhere around 1553, the short book appeared in English under the wonderfully old-school title *The Goodli History of the Moste Noble and Beautyfull Ladye Lucres of Scene in Tuskane, and of Her Louer Eurialus Verye Pleasaunt and Delectable vnto ye Reder*. Despite the obvious historical interest of this archaic Vatican porn, it has never been translated into contemporary language. (The passages quoted below mark the first time that any of the book has appeared in modern English.)

The 1400s being what they were, the action is pretty tame by today's standards. At one point, Euralius scales a wall to be with Lucres: "When she saw her lover, she clasped him in her arms. There was embracing and kissing, and with full sail they followed their lusts and wearied Venus, now with Ceres, and now with Bacchus was refreshed." Loosely translated, that last part means that they shagged, then ate, then drank wine.

His Holiness describes the next time they hook up:

Thus talking to each other, they went into the bedroom, where they had such a night as we judge the two lovers Paris and Helen had after he had taken her away, and it was so pleasant that they thought Mars and Venus had never known such pleasure....

Her mouth, and now her eyes, and now her cheeks he kissed. Pulling down her clothes, he saw such beauty as he had never seen before. "I have found more, I believe," said Euralius, "than Acteon saw of Diana when she bathed in the fountain. What is more pleasant or more fair than these limbs?... O fair neck and pleasant breasts, is it you that I touch? Is it you that I have? Are you in my hands? O round limbs, O sweet body, do I have you in my arms?... O pleasant kisses, O dear embraces, O sweet bites, no man alive is happier than I am, or more blessed."...

He strained, and she strained, and when they were done they weren't weary. Like Athens, who rose from the ground stronger, soon after battle they were more desirous of war.

But Euralius isn't just a horndog. He waxes philosophical about love to Lucres' cousin-in-law:

You know that man is prone to love. Whether it is virtue or vice, it reigns everywhere. No heart of flesh hasn't sometime felt the pricks of love. You know that neither the wise Solomon nor the strong Sampson has escaped from this passion. Furthermore, the nature of a kindled heart and a foolish love is this: The more it is allowed, the more it burns, with nothing sooner healing this than the obtaining of the loved. There have been many, both in our time and that of our elders, whose foolish love has been the cause of cruel death. And many who, after sex and love vouchsafed, have stopped burning. Nothing is better when love has crept into your bones than to give in to the burning, for those who strive against the tempest often wreck, while those who drive with the storm escape.

Besides sex and wisdom, the story also contains a lot of humor, as when Lucres' husband borrows a horse from Euralius: "He says to himself, 'If you leap upon my horse, I shall do the same thing to your wife.'"

Popes just don't write books like that anymore! ☐

03
THE CIA COMMITS OVER 100,000
SERIOUS CRIMES EACH YEAR

It's no big secret that the Central Intelligence Agency breaks the law. But just how often its does so is a shocker. A Congressional report reveals that the CIA's spooks "engage in highly illegal activities" at least *100,000* times each year (which breaks down to hundreds of crimes every day). Mind you, we aren't talking about run-of-the-mill illegal activities — these are "highly illegal activities" that "break extremely serious laws."

In 1996, the House of Representatives' Permanent Select Committee on Intelligence released a huge report entitled "IC21: The Intelligence Community in the 21st Century." Buried amid hundreds of pages is a single, devastating paragraph:

The CS [clandestine service] is the only part of the IC [intelligence community], indeed of the government, where hundreds of employees on a daily basis are directed to break extremely serious laws in countries around the world in the face of frequently sophisticated efforts by foreign governments to catch them. A safe estimate is that several hundred times every day (easily 100,000 times a year) DO [Directorate of Operations] officers engage in highly illegal activities (according to foreign law) that not only risk political embarrassment to the US but also endanger the freedom if not lives of the participating foreign nationals and, more than occasionally, of the clandestine officer himself.

Amazingly, there is no explanation, no follow-up. The report simply drops this bombshell and moves on as blithely as if it had just printed a grocery list.

One of the world's foremost experts on the CIA — John Kelly, who uncovered this revelation — notes that this is "the first official admission and definition of CIA covert operations as crimes." He goes on to say:

The report suggested that the CIA's crimes include murder and that "the targets of the CS [Clandestine Service] are increasingly international and transnational and a global presence is increasingly crucial to attack those targets." In other words, we are not talking about simply stealing secrets. We are talking about the CIA committing crimes against humanity with de facto impunity and congressional sanctioning.

Other government documents, including CIA reports, show that the CIA's crimes include terrorism, assassination, torture, and systematic violations of human rights. The documents also show that these crimes are part and parcel of deliberate CIA policy (the [congressional] report notes that CIA personnel are "directed" to commit crimes). ⵚ

04
THE FIRST CIA AGENT TO DIE IN THE LINE OF DUTY WAS DOUGLAS MACKIERNAN

As of the year 2000, 69 CIA agents had died in the line of duty. Of these, the identities of 40 remain classified. Former *Washington Post* and *Time* reporter Ted Gup spent three years tracking down information about these mysterious spooks who gave their lives for the Agency. (His resulting publication, *The Book of Honor*, names almost all of them.)

The first to die was Douglas Mackiernan. Undercover as a State Department diplomat, the US Army Air Corps Major worked in the capital of China's Xinjiang (Sinkiang) province, which Gup says "was widely regarded as the most remote and desolate consulate on earth." He went there in May 1947 to keep an eye on China's border with the Soviet Union and to monitor the Russkies' atomic tests.

In late September 1949, during the Communist takeover of China, Mackiernan left, but it was too late to use normal routes. Incredibly, he decided to go by foot during winter all the way to India, which would take him across a desert *and* the Himalayas. He, three White Russians, and a Fulbright scholar slogged the 1,000-mile trek in eight months. On April 29, 1950, they managed to reach the border of Tibet, but guards there thought the men were commies or bandits, and opened fire on them.

Hitting the ground, the bedraggled travelers waved a white flag, which stopped the gunfire. They slowly walked toward the border guards with their hands over their heads, but the Tibetans shot them, killing Mackiernan and two of the Russians. To add insult to injury, the guards cut the heads off the corpses. Their remains are buried at that spot.

With documents from the National Archives, Mackiernan's widow, and other sources, Gup pulled the CIA's first casualty out of the classified shadows. To this day, the Agency refuses to acknowledge Mackiernan's existence. ⌑

05
AFTER 9/11, THE DEFENSE DEPARTMENT WANTED TO POISON AFGHANISTAN'S FOOD SUPPLY

One of the strangest things the media do is to bury huge revelations deep in the bowels of a larger story. A perfect example occurs in "10 Days in September," an epic eight-day series that ran in the *Washington Post*. In part six, Bob Woodward and Dan Balz are recounting the Bush Administration's activities on September 17, 2001, six days after the 9/11 attacks. Bush and National Security Advisor Condoleezza Rice have headed to the Pentagon to be briefed on action against Afghanistan by a two-star general from the Special Operation Command:

Rice and Frank Miller, the senior NSC staffer for defense, went with the president to the Pentagon. Before the briefing, Miller reviewed the classified slide presentation prepared for Bush and got a big surprise.

One slide about special operations in Afghanistan said: Thinking Outside the

Box — Poisoning Food Supply. Miller was shocked and showed it to Rice. The United States doesn't know how to do this, Miller reminded her, and we're not allowed. It would effectively be a chemical or biological attack — clearly banned by treaties that the United States had signed, including the 1972 Biological Weapons Convention.

Rice took the slide to Rumsfeld. "This slide is not going to be shown to the president of the United States," she said.

Rumsfeld agreed. "You're right," he said.

Pentagon officials said later that their own internal review had caught the offending slide and that it never would have been shown to the president or to Rumsfeld. ♡

06
THE US GOVERNMENT LIES ABOUT THE NUMBER OF TERRORISM CONVICTIONS IT OBTAINS

Naturally enough, the Justice Department likes to trumpet convictions of terrorists. Besides garnering great publicity and allowing the citizenry to sleep snugly at night, this means more money for the department. The problem is that the numbers are a sham.

The story broke when the *Philadelphia Inquirer* examined convictions that the Justice Department said involved terrorism during the five year-period ending September 30, 2001. They found ludicrous examples of misclassification:

In one vivid example, an assistant US attorney in San Francisco asked US District Judge Marilyn H. Patel on Monday to stiffen a sentence against an Arizona man who got drunk on a United Airlines flight from Shanghai, repeatedly rang the call button, demanded more liquor, and put his hands on a flight attendant. Justice Department records show the case as "domestic terrorism."

In another case: "A tenant fighting eviction called his landlord, impersonated an FBI agent, and said the bureau did not want the tenant evicted. The landlord recognized the man's voice and called the real FBI."

Other "terrorist" incidents included prisoners rioting for better food, "the former court employee who shoved and threatened a judge," and "[s]even Chinese sailors [who] were convicted of taking over a Taiwanese fishing boat and sailing to the US territory of Guam, where they hoped to win political asylum."

After this chicanery was exposed, Republican Congressman Dan Burton asked the General Accounting Office — a nonpartisan governmental unit that investigates matters for Congress — to look into the Justice Department's claims of terrorist convictions. Sure enough, the GAO reported that the situation isn't nearly as rosy as we've been told.

In the year after 9/11 — from September 30, 2001, to that date the following year — the Justice Department maintained that 288 terrorists had been convicted in the US of their heinous crimes. But the GAO found that at least 132 of these cases (approximately 42 percent) had *nothing* to do with terrorism. Because of the GAO's methodology, it didn't verify every one of the remaining 156 convictions, so it refers to their accuracy as "questionable."

The deception is even worse when you zoom in on the cases classified as "international terrorism," which are the most headline-grabbing of all. Out of 174 such convictions, 131 (an amazing 75 percent) weren't really about terror.

After all of this humiliation, the Justice Department must've cleaned up its act, right? That's what it told the *Philadelphia Inquirer*. Well, the paper did a follow-up on "terrorism" cases for the first two months of 2003. Out of the 56 federal cases supposedly involving terrorism, at least 41 were bogus. Eight of them involved Puerto Ricans protesting the Navy's use of Vieques as a bombing range. The prosecutor who handled these cases says she doesn't know why they were classified as terrorism. Similarly, 28 Latinos were arrested for working at airports with phony ID, and a spokesman for the US Attorney says they weren't even suspected of being involved in terrorism. The most ridiculous example: "A Middle Eastern man indicted in Detroit for allegedly passing bad checks who has the same name as a Hezbollah leader." ⌁

07
THE US IS PLANNING TO *PROVOKE* TERRORIST ATTACKS

Perhaps the government won't need to inflate its terrorism-arrest stats after it implements the Defense Science Board's recommendation. This influential committee inside the Pentagon has proposed a terrifying way to fight evil-doers: Goad them into making terrorist attacks. Yes, you read correctly. Instead of waiting for a plot to be hatched and possibly executed, go out and *make* it happen.

In summer 2002, the Defense Science Board outlined all kinds of ways to fight the war on terrorism around the world. The scariest suggestion involves the creation of a new 100-man, $100-million team called the Proactive Pre-emptive Operations Group, or P2OG.

This combination of elite special forces soldiers and intelligence agents will have "an entirely new capability to proactively, pre-emptively provoke responses from adversary/terrorist groups," according to the DSB's report.

Just how the P2OG will "provoke" terrorists into action is not specified, at least in the unclassified portions of the report. United Press International — which apparently has access to the full, classified version of the report — says that techniques could include "stealing their money or tricking them with fake communications." The *Moscow Times* offers further possibilities, such as killing family members and infiltrating the groups with provocateurs, who will suggest and even direct terrorist strikes.

Once the terrorists have been provoked, what then? UPI says that by taking action, the terrorists would be "exposing themselves to 'quick-response' attacks by US forces." In other words, the plan is to hit the hornet's nest with a stick, while waiting nearby with a can of bug spray. The flaws in this approach are obvious. Although not spelled out in the UPI article or the report itself, the idea seems to be that the P2OG will cause terrorists to make an attack but supposedly stop them right before the attack actually occurs. Will the P2OG always be able to prevent terrorism it creates from taking place? Will it always be able to "neutralize" all of the terrorists during that crucial window after a plan has been put into motion but before it's been carried out? I wouldn't want to bet lives on it. But that's exactly what's happening.

Whenever any future terrorist attack occurs — an embassy is truck-bombed, a nightclub is blown to smithereens, prominent buildings are hit with hijacked passenger jets — we'll never be 100 percent sure that this wasn't an operation the P2OG provoked but then was unable to stop in time. ▢

08
THE US AND SOVIET UNION CONSIDERED DETONATING NUCLEAR BOMBS ON THE MOON

You'd be forgiven for thinking that this is an unused scene from *Dr. Strangelove*, but the United States and the Soviet Union have seriously considered exploding atomic bombs on the Moon.

It was the late 1950s, and the Cold War was extremely chilly. Someone in the US government got the bright idea of nuking the Moon, and in 1958 the Air Force Special Weapons Center spearheaded the project (labeled A119, "A Study of Lunar Research Flights").

The idea was to shock and awe the Soviet Union, and everybody else, with a massive display of American nuclear might. What better demonstration than an atomic explosion on our closest celestial neighbor? According to the project's reports, the flash would've been visible to the naked eye on Earth. (It's been suggested that another motivation may have been to use the Moon as a test range, thus avoiding the problems with irradiating our home planet.)

Carl Sagan was among the scientists lending his intellectual muscle to this hare-brained scheme. The project's leader was physicist Leonard Reiffel, who said: "I made it clear at the time there would be a huge cost to science of destroying a pristine lunar environment, but the US Air Force were mainly concerned about how the nuclear explosion would play on earth."

When a reporter for Reuters asked him what had happened to Project A119, Reiffel replied, "After the final report in early- to mid-1959, it simply went away, as things sometimes do in the world of classified activities."

Astoundingly, this wasn't the only time that a nuclear strike on the Moon was contemplated. Science reporter Keay Davidson reveals that "in 1956, W.W. Kellogg of RAND Corporation considered the possibility of launching an atomic bomb to the Moon." In 1957, NASA's Jet Propulsion Laboratory put forth Project Red Socks, the first serious proposal to send spacecraft to the Moon. One of its lesser suggestions was to nuke the Moon in order to send lunar rocks hurtling back to Earth, where they could be collected and studied. The following year, the leading American astronomer of the time, Gerard Kuiper, coauthored a memo which considered the scientific advantages of nuking the Moon. The creator of the hydrogen bomb, physicist Edward Teller, similarly mused about dropping atomic bombs on the Moon in order to study the seismic waves they would create.

The Soviet Union got in on the act, also in the late 1950s. Project E-4 would've used a probe armed with an A-bomb to blast the Moon, apparently as a display of one-upmanship. The idea reached the stage of a full-scale model but was aborted for fear of the probe falling back to Earth. ▢

09
TWO ATOMIC BOMBS WERE DROPPED ON NORTH CAROLINA

Fortunately, no atomic bombs were dropped on the Moon, but the same can't be said of North Carolina. The Tar Heel State's brush with nuclear catastrophe came on January 24, 1961, about half past midnight. A B-52 with two nukes on-board was cruising the skies near Goldsboro and Faro when its right wing leaked fuel and exploded. The jet disintegrated. Five crewmen survived, while three died.

The two MARK 39 thermonuclear bombs disengaged from the jet. Each one had a yield of two to four megatons (reports vary), up to 250 times as powerful as the bomb that decimated

Hiroshima. The parachute opened on one of them, and it drifted to the earth relatively gently. But the parachute failed to open on the other, so it plowed into a marshy patch of land owned by a farmer.

The nuke with the parachute was recovered easily. However, its twin proved much more difficult to retrieve. Because of the swampiness of the area, workers were able to drag out only part of the bomb. One of its most crucial components — the "secondary," which contains nuclear material — is still in the ground, probably around 150 feet down.

The federal government bought rights to this swatch of land to prevent any owners from digging more than five feet under the surface. To this day, state regulators test the radiation levels of the ground water in the area every year. The head of the North Carolina Division of Radiation Protection has said that they've found only normal levels but that "there is still an open question as to whether a hazard exists."

The big question is whether or not North Carolina's own Fat Man and Little Boy could've actually detonated. Due to the technicalities of nuclear weapons — and the ambiguous nature of the terms "unarmed," "armed," and "partially armed" — it's hard to give a definitive answer. We do know this: The Defense Department said that the ill-fated B-52 was part of a program (since discontinued) that continuously kept nuclear bombs in the air, ready for dropping. So, the answer is yes, that jet was fully capable of unleashing its A-bombs in completely armed mode, with all that this implies — mushroom clouds, vaporized people, dangerous radiation levels for decades, etc.

According to the late Chuck Hansen — one of the world's leading authorities on nuclear weapons — the pilot of the B-52 would've had to throw a switch to arm the bombs. Since he didn't, the bombs couldn't have gone off. Hansen mentions the possibility that the switch could've been activated while the jet was breaking apart and exploding. Luckily this didn't happen, but it was a possibility.

That switch apparently was the only thing that stopped the bombs from turning part of North Carolina into toast. The government's own reports show that for both bombs, *three* of the four arming devices had activated. Former Secretary of Defense Robert McNamara further corroborated this during a press conference, saying that the nukes "went through all but one" of the necessary steps.

Hansen told college students researching this near-miss:

This was a very dangerous incident and I suspect that steps were taken afterwards to prevent any repetition of it. I do not now know of any other weapon accident that came this close to a full-scale nuclear detonation (which is not to say that any such incident did not occur later).

10
WORLD WAR III ALMOST STARTED IN 1995

What were you doing on January 25, 1995? Whatever it was, it was almost the last thing you ever did. On that day, the world came within minutes of a nuclear war between the US and Russia.

Norway and the United States had launched a research rocket (for charting the Arctic) from a Norwegian island. Following standard protocol, Norway had alerted Russia in advance about the firing, but the message never made its way to the right people. In the middle of the night, Russian radar detected what looked like a nuclear missile launched toward Moscow from a US submarine.

The military immediately called President Boris Yeltsin, awakening him with the news that the country appeared to be under attack (no word on whether Yeltsin had been in a vodka-induced drunken slumber). The groggy president, for the first time ever, activated the infamous black suitcase that contains the codes for launching nuclear missiles. He had just a few minutes to decide whether to launch any or all of the country's 2,000 hair-trigger nukes at the US.

Luckily for the entire world, while Yeltsin was conferring with his highest advisors, Russia's radar showed that the missile was headed out to sea. The red alert was cancelled. World War III was averted.

What makes this even more nerve-racking is that Russia's early-warning systems are in much worse shape now than they were in '95. The Institute of Electrical and Electronic Engineers explains that while Russia needs 21 satellites to have a complete, fully-redundant network capable of accurately detecting missile launches, as of 1999 they have only three. Heaven help us if some Russian bureaucrat again forgets to tell the command and control center that a nearby country is launching a research rocket. ⛢

11
THE KOREAN WAR NEVER ENDED

Better not tell Hawkeye Pierce and the rest of the gang from *M*A*S*H*, but the Korean War is technically still happening. This comes to us from no less an authority than Howard S. Levie, the man who drafted the Korean Armistice Agreement. At the time, this law professor was a captain in the Office of the Judge Advocate General (JAG). He explains:

An armistice is not a peace treaty. While its main objective is to bring about a cease-fire, a halt to hostilities, that halt may be indefinite or for a specified period of time only. An armistice agreement does not terminate the state of war between the belligerents. A state of war continues to exist with all of its implications for the belligerents and for the neutrals.

The Korean Armistice itself even specifies that it is only a stop-gap measure "until a final peaceful settlement is achieved." To date, this settlement — otherwise known as a peace treaty — has never occurred. One attempt was made, at the Geneva Convention of 1954, but nothing came of it.

Interestingly, the Armistice wasn't signed at all by South Korea but rather by the head honchos in the United Nations Command, North Korea's army, and China's army. It should also be noted that the conflict in Korea wasn't technically a "war," because — like so many other post-WWII hostilities — there was no formal declaration of war. As *The Korean War: An Encyclopedia* trenchantly observes: "Since the war had never been declared, it was fitting that there should be no official ending, merely a suspension of hostilities."

North Korea has more than once denounced the Armistice, threatening to press the "play" button on the long-paused Korean War. Most recently, in February 2003, Kim Jong-il's government said that because of repeated US violations, the Armistice is merely "a blank piece of paper without any effect or significance." ␡

12
AGENT ORANGE WAS USED IN KOREA

"Agent Orange" is practically synonymous with the Vietnam War. The Dow Chemical defoliant was used to de-junglize large areas, exposing enemy troops, supplies, and infiltrators. It has been linked, though never definitively, to a number of nasty health problems such as Hodgkin's disease and adult-onset diabetes, plus spina bifida in offspring. The Veterans Administration compensates sick veterans who were exposed in Vietnam.

But it turns out that 'Nam wasn't the only place to get doused with this super-herbicide. From April 1968 to July 1969, 21,000 gallons of Agent Orange were sprayed along a strip of land abutting the southern border of the Demilitarized Zone between the two Koreas. During that time period, around 80,000 US military personnel served in South Korea, although not all of them would've been in the vicinity of the DMZ. The VA contradicts itself regarding who did the spraying, claiming at one point that it was South Korea but saying at another that the Department of Defense did it.

In September 2000, the VA quietly sent letters to veterans who served in Korea during the spraying, letting them know that they may have been dosed with Agent Orange. Since these letters were sent over 30 years after the exposure, the Pentagon must've just found out about it, right? Actually, even if you buy the story that the South Koreans were responsible, the US military knew about the spraying at the time it happened but kept quiet about it for decades. It was only when news reports began citing declassified documents in 1999 that the government decided to do something.

Possibly exposed vets can get tested for free by the Veterans Administration. The catch is, if they're sick with Hodgkin's or some other horrible disease, they — unlike their Vietnam compatriots — aren't eligible for compensation or additional health care. However, for their agony, Korean vets will receive a free newsletter, the same one that Vietnam vets get. ⛶

13
KENT STATE WASN'T THE ONLY — OR EVEN THE FIRST — MASSACRE OF COLLEGE STUDENTS DURING THE VIETNAM ERA

It's one of the defining moments of the Vietnam era and, more than that, twentieth-century US history in general. On May 4, 1970, the Ohio National Guard opened fire on unarmed Kent State University students protesting the war. Four were killed, eight were wounded, and another was left paralyzed. It's so ingrained in the country's psyche that it even appears in American history textbooks, and the anniversary is noted each year by the major media.

Yet this wasn't the only time the authorities slaughtered unarmed college kids during this time period. It happened on at least two other occasions, which have been almost completely forgotten.

A mere ten days after the Kent State massacre, students at the historically black Jackson State University in Mississippi were protesting not only the Vietnam War and the recent killings at Kent, but racism as well. On the night of May 14, 1970, during the protests, a small riot broke out when a false rumor swept the campus: The black mayor of Fayette, Mississippi, was said to have been assassinated. As at Kent State, some students or provocateurs threw bricks and stones and set fires. Firefighters trying to put out a blaze in a men's dorm were hassled by an angry crowd, so they called for police protection. The campus was cordoned off.

Jackson State's Website devoted to the incident says: "Seventy-five city policemen and Mississippi State Police officers armed with carbines, submachine guns, shotguns, service revolvers and some personal weapons, responded to the call." After the fire had been extinguished, the heavily armed cops marched down the street, herding students towards a women's dorm. As the Website notes: "No one seems to know why."

Seventy-five to 100 students were pushed back until they were in front of the dorm, where they began yelling and throwing things at the police. "Accounts disagree as to what happened next. Some students said the police advanced in a line, warned them, then opened fire. Others said the police abruptly opened fire on the crowd and the dormitory. Other witnesses reported that the students were under the control of a campus security officer when the police opened fire. Police claimed they spotted a powder flare in the Alexander West Hall third floor stairwell window and opened fire in self-defense on the dormitory only. Two local television news reporters present at the shooting agreed that a shot was fired, but were uncertain of the direction. A radio reporter claimed to have seen an arm and a pistol extending from a dormitory window."

Two people — both outside the dorm — were killed in over 30 seconds of sustained gunfire from the cops. Jackson student Phillip Lafayette Gibbs was shot in the head, and a bystander — high-school senior James Earl Green — took it in the chest. A dozen students were nonfatally shot, and many more were injured by flying glass. Over 460 rounds had hit the dorm. No member of law enforcement was injured.

After the carnage, Inspector "Goon" Jones radioed the dispatcher, saying that "nigger students" had been killed. When the dispatcher asked him about the injured, he said: "I think there are about three more nigger males there…. There were two nigger gals — two more nigger gals from over there shot in the arm, I believe."

Even less known is the Orangeburg massacre, which took place two years earlier. Students at South Carolina State University in Orangeburg — joined by students from another black college, Claflin University — were protesting the failure of the town's only bowling alley to racially integrate. February 8, 1968, was the fourth night of demonstrations, and students had lit a bonfire on campus. Police doused it, but a second one was started. When the cops tried to extinguish this one, the crowd — in a scene to be replayed at Kent and Jackson — started throwing things at them. One highway patrolmen fired warning shots into the air, and all hell broke loose as the assembled police opened fire on the unarmed crowd.

After a barrage of weapons-fire, three people were dead — eighteen-year-olds Henry Smith and Samuel Hammond, and high-school student Delano Middleton. Twenty-seven other demonstrators were wounded. The vast majority of them had been shot in the back as they ran away.

South Carolina's Governor praised the police for their handling on the situation, giving all of them promotions. Nine patrolmen were eventually tried on federal charges, and all were acquitted. It was only 33 years later — on the 2001 anniversary of the carnage — that a Governor of the state admitted the heinous nature of what happened that night. Governor Jim Hodges said, "We deeply regret" the mass-shooting, but he stopped short of apologizing for it. ⌗

14
WINSTON CHURCHILL BELIEVED IN
A WORLDWIDE JEWISH CONSPIRACY

ILLUSTRATED SUNDAY HERALD, FEBRUARY 8, 1920.   Page 5.

ZIONISM versus BOLSHEVISM.
A STRUGGLE FOR THE SOUL OF THE JEWISH PEOPLE.
By the Rt. Hon. WINSTON S. CHURCHILL.

Like Henry Ford, Britain's larger-than-life wartime Prime Minister, Winston Churchill, believed that a group of "international Jews" was striving to take over the world. On February 8, 1920, the *Illustrated Sunday Herald* (published in London) ran an article by Churchill. Its title: "Zionism Versus Bolshevism: A Struggle for the Soul of the Jewish People." At the time, Winnie was Secretary of State for War and Air and had already been a prominent Member of Parliament.

Churchill didn't slam all Jews; rather, he painted them as a people of two extremes. "The conflict between good and evil which proceeds unceasingly in the breast of man nowhere reaches such an intensity as in the Jewish race. The dual nature of mankind is nowhere more strongly or more terribly exemplified…. It would almost seem as if the gospel of Christ and the gospel of Antichrist were destined to originate among the same people; and that this mystic and mysterious race had been chosen for the supreme manifestations, both of the divine and the diabolical."

He identifies three strains of political thought among the world's Jews: Nationalism, in which a

Jewish person identifies first and foremost with the country in which he or she lives. Zionism, in which a Jewish person wants a country specifically for Jews (Israel would be formed 28 years after Winnie's essay). These are both honorable, says Churchill, unlike the third option — the terrorism and atheistic communism of "International Jews." He writes:

International Jews
In violent opposition to all this sphere of Jewish effort rise the schemes of the International Jews. The adherents of this sinister confederacy are mostly men reared up among the unhappy populations of countries where Jews are persecuted on account of their race. Most, if not all, of them have forsaken the faith of their forefathers, and divorced from their minds all spiritual hopes of the next world. This movement among the Jews is not new. From the days of Spartacus-Weishaupt to those of Karl Marx, and down to Trotsky (Russia), Bela Kun (Hungary), Rosa Luxembourg (Germany), and Emma Goldman (United States), this world-wide conspiracy for the overthrow of civilization and for the reconstitution of society on the basis of arrested development, of envious malevolence, and impossible equality, has been steadily growing. It played, as a modern writer, Mrs. Webster, has so ably shown, a definitely recognizable part in the tragedy of the French Revolution. It has been the mainspring of every subversive movement during the Nineteenth Century; and now at last this band of extraordinary personalities from the underworld of the great cities of Europe and America have gripped the Russian people by the hair of their heads and have become practically the undisputed masters of that enormous empire.

Terrorist Jews

There is no need to exaggerate the part played in the creation of Bolshevism and in the actual bringing about of the Russian Revolution, by these international and for the most part atheistical Jews, it is certainly a very great one; it probably outweighs all others. With the notable exception of Lenin, the majority of the leading figures are Jews. Moreover, the principal inspiration and driving power comes from the Jewish leaders. Thus Tchitcherin, a pure Russian, is eclipsed by his nominal subordinate Litvinoff, and the influence of Russians like Bukharin or Lunacharski cannot be compared with the power of Trotsky, or of Zinovieff, the Dictator of the Red Citadel (Petrograd) or of Krassin or Radek — all Jews. In the Soviet institutions the predominance of Jews is even more astonishing. And the prominent, if not indeed the principal, part in the system of terrorism applied by the Extraordinary Commissions for Combating Counter-Revolution has been taken by Jews, and in some notable cases by Jewesses. The same evil prominence was obtained by Jews in the brief period of terror during which Bela Kun ruled in Hungary. The same phenomenon has been presented in Germany (especially in Bavaria), so far as this madness has been allowed to prey upon the temporary prostration of the German people. Although in all these countries there are many non-Jews every whit as bad as the worst of the Jewish revolutionaries, the part played by the latter in proportion to their numbers in the population is astonishing.

Naturally, Churchill's admirers aren't exactly proud of this essay, which has led some of them to question its authenticity. However, the leading Churchill bibliographer, Frederick Woods, has pronounced the article genuine, listing it in his authoritative *A Bibliography of the Works of Sir Winston Churchill.* ⌻

15
THE AUSCHWITZ TATTOO WAS ORIGINALLY AN IBM CODE NUMBER

The tattooed numbers on the forearms of people held and killed in Nazi concentration camps have become a chilling symbol of hatred. Victims were stamped with the indelible number in a dehumanizing effort to keep track of them like widgets in the supply chain.

These numbers obviously weren't chosen at random. They were part of a coded system, with each number tracked as the unlucky person who bore it was moved through the system.

Edwin Black made headlines in 2001 when his painstakingly researched book, *IBM and the Holocaust*, showed that IBM machines were used to automate the "Final Solution" and the jackbooted takeover of Europe. Worse, he showed that the top levels of the company either knew or willfully turned a blind eye.

A year and a half after that book gave Big Blue a black eye, the author made more startling discoveries. IBM equipment was on-site at the Auschwitz concentration camp. Furthermore:

Thanks to the new discoveries, researchers can now trace how Hollerith numbers

assigned to inmates evolved into the horrific tattooed numbers so symbolic of the Nazi era. (Herman Hollerith was the German American who first automated US census information in the late 19th century and founded the company that became IBM. Hollerith's name became synonymous with the machines and the Nazi "departments" that operated them.) In one case, records show, a timber merchant from Bendzin, Poland, arrived at Auschwitz in August 1943 and was assigned a characteristic five-digit IBM Hollerith number, 44673. The number was part of a custom punch-card system devised by IBM to track prisoners in all Nazi concentration camps, including the slave labor at Auschwitz. Later in the summer of 1943, the Polish timber merchant's same five-digit Hollerith number, 44673, was tattooed on his forearm. Eventually, during the summer of 1943, all non-Germans at Auschwitz were similarly tattooed.

The Hollerith numbering system was soon scrapped at Auschwitz because so many inmates died. Eventually, the Nazis developed their own haphazard system. ♔

16
ADOLPH HITLER'S BLOOD RELATIVES ARE ALIVE AND WELL IN NEW YORK STATE

Adolph Hitler never had kids, so we tend to take for granted the idea that no one alive is closely related to him. But historians have long known that he had a nephew who was born in Britain and moved to the United States. Alois Hitler, Jr., was Adolph's older half-brother (their common parent was Alois Sr.). Alois Jr. — a waiter in Dublin — married an Irish woman, and, after moving to Liverpool, they had a son, William Patrick Hitler.

Pat, as he was called, moved to Germany as a young adult to take advantage of his uncle's rising political stature, but Adolph just gave him minor jobs and kept him out of the limelight. After being subtly threatened by Rudolph Hess to become a German citizen, and having gotten tired of being dissed by Adolph, Pat came to America in 1939 and went on a lecture tour around the US, denouncing his uncle. (For his part, Adolph referred to his nephew as "loathsome.") While World War II was raging, Pat joined the US Navy, so he could fight against Uncle Adolph. Afterwards, he changed his last name, and this is where the trail goes cold.

That is, until US-based British reporter David Gardner was assigned to track down and interview William Patrick. Originally given two weeks to file the story, Gardner realized that finding Hitler's long-lost nephew was tougher than it first appeared. He worked on the story during his spare time for several years, unearthing old news clippings, filing requests for government documents, interviewing possible relatives, and chasing a lot of dead ends.

He finally discovered that William Patrick had ended up in a small town in Long Island, New York. Pat had died in 1987, but Gardner showed up unannounced on the doorstep of his widow, Phyllis, who confirmed that her late husband was Adolph Hitler's nephew. She also mentioned that she and Pat had sons, but she quickly clammed up and asked Gardner to leave. The two never spoke again.

After more legwork, Gardner found that Pat and Phyllis produced four children, all sons. The eldest, born in 1949, is named Alexander Adolph. (Just why Pat would name his firstborn after his detested uncle is one of many mysteries still surrounding the Hitler kin.) Then came Louis in 1951, Howard (1957), and Brian (1965). Howard — a fraud investigator for the IRS — died in a car crash in 1989, and Louis and Brian continue to run a landscaping business in the small New York community. Alex lives in a larger Long Island city. He twice spoke to Gardner but didn't reveal very much, saying that the family's ancestry is "a pain in the ass." Alex said that his brothers made a pact never to have children, in order to spare their progeny the burden of being related to a monster. He denied having made such a vow himself, despite the fact that he is still childless.

Gardner sums it up: "Although there are some distant relations living equally quiet lives in Austria, the three American sons are the only descendants of the paternal line of the family. They are, truly, the last of the Hitlers." ⊐

17
AROUND ONE QUARTER OF "WITCHES" WERE MEN

The word "witch" has become synonymous with "woman accused of working magic," and the consensus tells us that the witch trials in Europe and Colonial America were simply a war against women (ie, "gendercide"). Most popular works on the subject ignore the men who were accused and executed for supposedly practicing witchcraft. Academic works that don't omit male witches usually explain them away, as if they were just a few special cases that don't really count.

Into this gap step Andrew Gow, an associate professor of history at the University of Alberta, and one of his grad students, Lara Apps. Their book *Male Witches in Early Modern Europe* scours the literature and finds that, of the 110,000 people tried for witchcraft and the 60,000 executed from 1450 to 1750, somewhere between 20 to 25 percent were men.

This is an average across Europe, the British Isles, and the American Colonies; the gender ratios vary widely from place to place. The lowest percentages of males were persecuted in the Basel region of Switzerland (5 percent) and in Hungary (10 percent). Places that hovered around the 50/50 mark were Finland (49 percent) and Burgundy (52 percent). Men were the clear majority of "witches" in Estonia (60 percent) and Norway (73 percent). During Iceland's witch craze, from 1625 to 1685, an amazing 110 out of 120 "witches" were men, for a percentage of 92. As for America, almost a third of those executed during the infamous Salem witch trials (six out of nineteen) were men.

Besides bringing these numbers to light, professor Gow and pupil Apps present serious challenges to the attempts to erase male witches from the picture. For example, some writers claim that the men were caught up in the hysteria solely because they were related to accused women. In this scenario, the men were only "secondary targets" ("collateral damage," perhaps?). But in numerous instances men were persecuted by themselves. In other cases, a woman became a secondary target *after* her husband had been singled out as a witch.

Although women were the overall majority of victims, the "burning times" were pretty rough for men, too. ⌁

18
THE VIRGINIA COLONISTS PRACTICED CANNIBALISM

During the harsh winter of 1609-1610, British subjects in the famous colony of Jamestown, Virginia, ate their dead and their shit. This fact doesn't make it into very many US history textbooks, and the state's official Website apparently forgot to mention it in their history section.

When you think about it rationally, this fact should be a part of mainstream history. After all, it demonstrates the strong will to survive among the colonists. It shows the mind-boggling hardships they endured and overcame. Yet the taboo against eating these two items is so over-powering that this episode can't be mentioned in conventional history.

Luckily, an unconventional historian, Howard Zinn, revealed this fact in his classic *A People's History of the United States*. Food was so nonexistent during that winter, only 60 out of 500 colonists survived. A government document from that time gives the gruesome details:

Driven thru insufferable hunger to eat those things which nature most abhorred, the flesh and excrements of man as well of our own nation as of an Indian, digged by some out of his grave after he had lain buried three days and wholly devoured him; others, envying the better state of body of any whom hunger has not yet so much wasted as their own, lay wait and threatened to kill and eat them; one among them slew his wife as she slept in his bosom, cut her in pieces, salted her and fed upon her till he had clean devoured all parts saving her head. ⌖

19
MANY OF THE PIONEERING FEMINISTS OPPOSED ABORTION

The idea that feminism equals the right to an abortion has become so ingrained that it seems ludicrous to think otherwise. "Prolife feminism" appears to be an inherent contradiction in terms. Yet more than 20 founding mothers of the feminist movement — who helped secure women's rights to vote, to own property, to use contraception, to divorce abusive husbands — were adamantly opposed to abortion.

The most famous nineteenth-century feminist — Susan B. Anthony, she of the ill-fated dollar coin — referred to abortion as "the horrible crime of child-murder." And that's just for starters. She also called it "infanticide," "this most monstrous crime," "evil," and a "dreadful deed." Surprisingly, given that unsparing language, she didn't believe that it should be made illegal. Responding to an article in which a man called for the outlawing of abortion, Anthony writes: "Much as I deplore the horrible crime of child-murder, earnestly as I desire its suppression, I cannot believe with the writer of the above-mentioned article, that such a law would have the desired effect. It seems to be only mowing off the top of the noxious weed, while the root remains."

The root, she believed, was the horrible way in which women (and children) were treated. As summed up in the book *Prolife Feminism*, these pioneering women felt that "abortion was the product of a social system that compelled women to remain ignorant about their bodies, that enabled men to dominate them sexually without taking responsibility for the consequences, that denied women support during and after the resulting pregnancies, and that placed far more value on a child's 'legitimacy' than on his or her life and well-being."

Indeed, while Anthony gave women a lot of grief for ending a pregnancy, she reserved the most vitriol for the men who knocked them up:

Guilty? Yes, no matter what the motive, love of ease, or a desire to save from suffering the unborn innocent, the woman is awfully guilty who commits the deed. It will burden her conscience in life, it will burden her soul in death; but oh! thrice guilty is he who, for selfish gratification, heedless of her prayers, indifferent to her fate, drove her to the desperation which impelled her to her crime.

Elizabeth Cady Stanton, Anthony's best friend for life, resented society's dictate that all women must become mothers. Yet she also thought that "maternity is grand," but it must be on the woman's own terms. Despite this, she railed against abortion. Like her pal, she referred to abortions as "murder," "a crying evil," "abominations," and "revolting outrages against the laws of nature and our common humanity." Also like Anthony, Stanton laid the blame for abortion at the feet of men.

Dr. Elizabeth Blackwell, lionized as the first US woman to become a medical doctor (in 1849), wrote in her diary:

The gross perversion and destruction of motherhood by the abortionist filled me with indignation, and awakened active antagonism. That the honorable term "female physician" should be exclusively applied to those women who carried on this shocking trade seemed to me a horror. It was an utter degradation of what might and should become a noble position for women.

Another prolife feminist was Victoria Woodhull, best known for being the first female candidate for US President (way back in 1870). Radical even by early feminist standards, she and her sister, Tennessee Claflin, declared that children had rights which began at conception. Their essay "The Slaughter of the Innocents" first discusses the abominable death rate of children under five, then turns its sights on abortion:

We are aware that many women attempt to excuse themselves for procuring abortions, upon the ground that it is not murder. But the fact of resort to so weak an argument only shows the more palpably that they fully realize the enormity of the crime. Is it not equally destroying the would-be future oak, to crush the sprout before it pushes its head above the sod, as it is to cut down the sapling, or cut down the tree? Is it not equally to destroy life, to crush it in its very germ, and to take it when the germ has evolved to any given point in its line of development? Let those who can see any difference regarding the time when life, once begun, is taken, console themselves that they are not murderers having been abortionists.

20
BLACK PEOPLE SERVED IN THE CONFEDERATE ARMY

Like "prolife feminist," the phrase "black Confederate" seems like an oxymoron. But the record shows that many slaves and free blacks were a part of the South's military during the US Civil War.

None other than abolitionist Frederick Douglass, a former slave and one of the most prominent African Americans in history, declared:

There are at present moment [autumn 1861], many colored men in the Confederate Army doing duty not only as cooks, servants, and laborers, but as real soldiers, having musket on their shoulders and bullets in their pockets, ready to shoot down loyal troops and do all that soldiers may do to destroy the Federal government and build up that of the traitors and rebels.

In *Black Confederates and Afro-Yankees in Civil War Virginia*, Professor Ervin L. Jordan, Jr., writes:

Numerous black Virginians served with Confederate forces as soldiers, sailors, teamsters, spies, and hospital personnel.... I know of black Confederate sharp-shooters who saw combat during the 1862 Seven Days Campaign and [of] the existence of black companies [which] organized and drilled in Richmond in March-April 1865. Integrated companies of black and white hospital workers fought against the Union army in the Petersburg trenches during March 1865. There were

several recruitment campaigns and charity balls held in Virginia on behalf of black soldiers and special camps of instruction were established to train them.

The book *Black Confederates* contains loads of primary documents testifying to the role of African Americans: letters, military documents, tributes, obituaries, contemporaneous newspaper articles, and more. In an 1862 letter to his uncle, a soldier at Camp Brown in Knoxville, Tennessee, wrote that his company had recently gunned down six Union soldiers and that "Jack Thomas a colored person that belongs to our company killed one of them."

An 1861 article in the *Montgomery Advertiser* says: "We are informed that Mr. G.C. Hale, of Autauga County, yesterday tendered to Governor Moore the services of a company of negroes, to assist in driving back the horde of abolition sycophants who are now talking so flippantly of reducing to a conquered province the Confederate States of the South."

The obituary of black South Carolinian Henry Brown states that he had never been a slave and had served in three wars: the Mexican, the Spanish-American, and the Civil (on the side of the South). He was given a 21-gun salute at his funeral.

In 1890, black Union veteran Joseph T. Wilson wrote in his book, *The Black Phalanx: A History of the Negro Soldiers of the United States*, that New Orleans was home to two Native Guard regiments, which comprised 3,000 "colored men." Referring to these regiments in an 1898 book, Union Captain Dan Matson said: "Here is a strange fact. We find that the Confederates themselves first armed and mustered the Negro as a solider in the late war."

Most blacks in the Confederate Army, though, were in supporting roles such as cook, musician, nurse, and the catch-all "servant." However, a lot of them ended up fighting on the battlefield, even though the South didn't officially induct black soldiers until late in the conflict. And all of them — whether inducted or not, whether solider or some other position — were eligible for military pensions from several Southern states (including Tennessee and Mississippi), and records show that many of them signed up for these benefits.

A follow-up volume, *Black Southerners in Confederate Armies*, presents even more source documents. A book from 1866 contains the recollection of a Union man whose compatriot killed a black Confederate sniper "who, through his skill as a marksman, had done more injury to our men that any dozen of his white compeers…" Union documents show Henry Marshall, a black soldier with the 14th Kentucky Cavalry, being held in Northern prisoner of war camps. A pension document from South Carolina reveals that "a free Negro who volunteered" for the army served from August 1861 to the end of the war — over three and a half years. An obituary for George Mathewson says that the former slave received "a Cross of Honor for bravery in action," based on his role as standard-bearer.

The *New York Tribune* noted "that the Rebels organized and employed 'Negro troops' a full year before our government could be persuaded to do any thing of the sort." After the Battle of Gettysburg, the *New York Herald* reported: "Among the rebel prisoners who were marched through Gettysburg there were observed seven negroes in uniform and fully accoutered as soldiers."

An article from *Smithsonian* magazine relates: "A *New York Times* correspondent with Grant in 1863 wrote: 'The guns of the rebel battery were manned almost wholly by Negroes, a single white man, or perhaps two, directing operations.'"

While it certainly couldn't be said that African Americans played a major military role in the Southern army, they were definitely there. And some of them had even volunteered. ▢

21
ELECTRIC CARS HAVE BEEN AROUND SINCE THE 1880s

The car of the future runs completely on electricity. No more dependence on gas. No more choking the atmosphere with fumes. Whenever the possibility of electric cars is raised, the media and other commentators ooh and ahh over the potential. But this technology isn't futuristic — it's positively retro. Cars powered by electricity have been on the scene since the 1800s and actually *predate* gas-powered cars.

A blacksmith in Vermont — Thomas Davenport — built the first rotary electric motor in 1833 and used it to power a model train the next year. In the late 1830s, Scottish inventor Robert Davidson rigged a carriage with an electric motor powered by batteries. In his Pulitzer-nominated book *Taking Charge*, archaeology professor and technology historian Michael Brian Schiffer writes that this "was perhaps the first electric car."

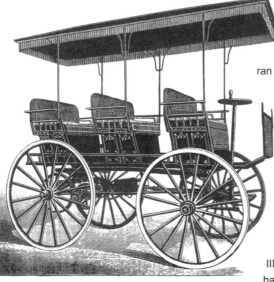

After this remarkable achievement, the idea of an electric car languished for decades. In 1881, a French experimenter debuted a personal vehicle that ran on electricity, a tricycle (ie, three wheels and a seat) for adults. In 1888, many inventors in the US, Britain, and Europe started creating three- and four-wheel vehicles — which could carry two to six people — that ran on electricity. These vehicles remained principally curiosities until May 1897, when the Pope Manufacturing Company — the country's most successful bicycle manufacturer — started selling the first commercial electric car: the Columbia Electric Phaeton, Mark III. It topped out at fifteen miles per hour, and had to be recharged every 30 miles. Within two years, people could choose from an array of electrical carriages, buggies, wagons, trucks, bicycles, tricycles, even buses and ambulances made by numerous manufacturers.

New York City was home to a fleet of electric taxi cabs starting in 1897. The Electric Vehicle Company eventually had over 100 of them ferrying people around the Big Apple. Soon it was unleashing electric taxis in Chicago, Philadelphia, Boston, and Washington DC. By 1900, though, the company was in trouble, and seven years later it sputtered out.

As for cars powered by dead dinosaurs, Austrian engineer Siegfried Marcus attached a one-cylinder motor to a cart in 1864, driving it 500 feet and thus creating the first vehicle powered by gas (this was around 25 years after Davidson had created the first electro-car). It wasn't until 1895 that gas autos — converted carriages with a two-cylinder engine — were commercially sold (and then only in microscopic numbers).

Around the turn of the century, the average car buyer had a big choice to make: gas, electric, or steam? When the auto industry took form around 1895, nobody knew which type of vehicle was going to become the standard. During the last few years of the nineteenth century and the first few of the twentieth, over 100 companies placed their bets on electricity. According to Schiffer, "Twenty-eight percent of the 4,192 American automobiles produced in 1900 were electric. In the New York automobile show of that year more electrics were on display than gasoline or steam vehicles."

In the middle of the first decade of the 1900s, electric cars were on the decline, and their gas-eating cousins were surging ahead. With improvements in the cars and their batteries, though, electrics started a comeback in 1907, which continued through 1913. The downhill slide started the next year, and by the 1920s the market for electrics was "minuscule," to use Schiffer's word. Things never got better.

Many companies tried to combine the best of both approaches, with cars that ran on a mix of electricity and gas. The Pope Manufacturing Company, once again in the vanguard, built a working prototype in 1898. A Belgian company and a French company each brought out commercial models the next year, beating the Toyota Prius and the Honda Insight to the market by over a century. Even Ferdinand Porsche and the Mercedes Company got in on the act. Unfortunately, these hybrids never really caught on.

Didik Design — which manufactures several vehicles which run on various combinations of electricity, solar power, and human power — maintains an extensive archive on the history of electric and electro-fuel cars. According to their research, around 200 companies and individuals have manufactured electric cars. Only a few familiar names are on the list (although some of them aren't familiar as car manufacturers): Studebaker (1952-1966), General Electric (1901-1904), Braun (1977), Sears, Roebuck, and Company (1978), and Oldsmobile (1896 to the present). The vast majority have long been forgotten: Elecctra, Pfluger, Buffalo Automobile Company, Hercules, Red Bug, and Nu-Klea Starlite, to name a few. Henry Ford and Thomas Edison teamed up on an electric car, but, although some prototypes were built, it never was commercially produced. Though they have faded from mass cultural memory, electric cars have never been completely out of production.

The reasons why electrics faded into obscurity while gas cars and trucks became 99.999 percent dominant are complex and are still being debated. If only they hadn't been sidelined and had continued to develop apace, the world would be a very different place. ▯

22
JURIES ARE ALLOWED TO JUDGE THE LAW, NOT JUST THE FACTS

In order to guard citizens against the whims of the King, the right to a trial by jury was established by the Magna Carta in 1215, and it has become one of the most sacrosanct legal aspects of British and American societies. We tend to believe that the duty of a jury is solely to determine whether someone broke the law. In fact, it's not unusual for judges to instruct juries that they are to judge only the facts in a case, while the judge will sit in judgment of the law itself. Nonsense.

Juries are the last line of defense against the power abuses of the authorities. They have the right to judge the law. Even if a defendant committed a crime, a jury can refuse to render a guilty verdict. Among the main reasons why this might happen, according to attorney Clay S. Conrad:

When the defendant has already suffered enough, when it would be unfair or against the public interest for the defendant to be convicted, when the jury disagrees with the law itself, when the prosecution or the arresting authorities have gone "too far" in the single-minded quest to arrest and convict a particular defendant, when the punishments to be imposed are excessive or when the jury suspects that the charges have been brought for political reasons or to make an unfair example of the hapless defendant...

Some of the earliest examples of jury nullification from Britain and the American Colonies were refusals to convict people who had spoken ill of the government (they were prosecuted under "seditious libel" laws) or who were practicing forbidden religions, such as Quakerism. Up to the time of the Civil War, American juries often refused to convict the brave souls who helped runaway slaves. In the 1800s, jury nullifications saved the hides of union organizers who were being prosecuted with conspiracy to restrain trade. Juries used their power to free people charged under the anti-alcohol laws of Prohibition, as well as antiwar protesters during the Vietnam era. Today, juries sometimes refuse to convict drug users (especially medical marijuana users), tax protesters, abortion protesters, gun owners, battered spouses, and people who commit "mercy killings."

Judges and prosecutors will often outright lie about the existence of this power, but centuries of court decisions and other evidence prove that jurors can vote their consciences.

When the US Constitution was created, with its Sixth Amendment guarantee of a jury trial, the most popular law dictionary of the time said that juries "may not only find things of their own knowledge, but they go according to their consciences." The first edition of Noah Webster's celebrated dictionary (1828) said that juries "decide both the law and the fact in criminal prosecutions."

Jury nullification is specifically enshrined in the constitutions of Pennsylvania, Indiana, and Maryland. The state codes of Connecticut and Illinois contain similar provisions.

The second US President, John Adams, wrote: "It is not only [the juror's] right, but his duty…to find the verdict according to his own best understanding, judgment, and conscience, though in direct opposition to the direction of the court." Similarly, Founding Father Alexander Hamilton declared: "It is essential to the security of personal rights and public liberty, that the jury should have and exercise the power to judge both of the law and of the criminal intent."

Legendary Supreme Court Chief Justice John Jay once instructed a jury:

It may not be amiss, here, Gentlemen, to remind you of the good old rule, that on questions of fact, it is the providence of the jury, on questions of law, it is the providence of the court to decide. But it must be observed that by the same law, which recognizes this reasonable distribution of jurisdiction, you have nevertheless the right to take upon yourselves to judge of both, and to determine the law as well as the fact in controversy.

The following year, 1795, Justice James Irdell declared: "[T]hough the jury will generally respect the sentiment of the court on points of law, they are not bound to deliver a verdict conformably to them." In 1817, Chief Justice John Marshall said that "the jury in a capital case were judges, as well of the law as the fact, and were bound to acquit where either was doubtful."

In more recent times, the Fourth Circuit Court of Appeals unanimously held in 1969:

If the jury feels that the law under which the defendant is accused is unjust, or that exigent circumstances justified the actions of the accused, or for any reason which appeals to their logic and passion, the jury has the power to

acquit, and the courts must abide that decision.

Three years later, the DC Circuit Court of Appeals noted: "The pages of history shine on instances of the jury's exercise of its prerogative to disregard uncontradicted evidence and instructions of the judge."

In a 1993 law journal article, federal Judge Jack B. Weinstein wrote: "When juries refuse to convict on the basis of what they think are unjust laws, they are performing their duties as jurors."

Those who try to wish away the power of jury nullification often point to cases in which racist juries have refused to convict white people charged with racial violence. As attorney Conrad shows in his book, *Jury Nullification: The Evolution of a Doctrine*, this has occurred only in very rare instances. Besides, it's ridiculous to try to stamp out or deny a certain power just because it can be used for bad ends as well as good. What form of power hasn't been misused at least once in a while?

The Fully Informed Jury Association (FIJA) is the best-known organization seeking to tell all citizens about their powers as jurors. People have been arrested for simply handing out FIJA literature in front of courthouses. During jury selections, FIJA members have been excluded solely on the grounds that they belong to the group.

FIJA also seeks laws that would require judges to tell jurors that they can and should judge the law, but this has been an uphill battle, to say the least. In a still-standing decision (*Sparf and Hansen v. US*, 1895), the Supreme Court ruled that judges don't have to let jurors know their full powers. In cases where the defense has brought up jury nullification during the proceedings, judges have sometimes held the defense attorney in contempt. Still, 21 state legislatures have introduced informed-jury legislation, with three of them passing it through one chamber (ie, House or Senate).

Quite obviously, the justice system is terrified of this power, which is all the more reason for us to know about it. ♋

23
THE POLICE AREN'T LEGALLY OBLIGATED TO PROTECT YOU

Without even thinking about it, we take it as a given that the police must protect each of us. That's their whole reason for existence, right?

While this might be true in a few jurisdictions in the US and Canada, it is actually the exception, not the rule. In general, court decisions and state laws have held that cops don't have to do a damn thing to help you when you're in danger.

In the only book devoted exclusively to the subject, *Dial 911 and Die*, attorney Richard W. Stevens writes:

It was the most shocking thing I learned in law school. I was studying Torts in my

first year at the University of San Diego School of Law, when I came upon the case of *Hartzler v. City of San Jose*. In that case I discovered the secret truth: *the government owes no duty to protect individual citizens from criminal attack*. Not only did the California courts hold to that rule, the California legislature had enacted a statute to make sure the courts couldn't change the rule.

But this doesn't apply to just the wild, upside down world of Kalifornia. Stevens cites laws and cases for every state — plus Washington DC, Puerto Rico, the Virgin Islands, and Canada — which reveal the same thing. If the police fail to protect you, even through sheer incompetence and negligence, don't expect that you or your next of kin will be able to sue.

Even in the nation's heartland, in bucolic Iowa, you can't depend on 911. In 1987, two men broke into a family's home, tied up the parents, slit the mother's throat, raped the 16-year-old daughter, and drove off with the 12-year old daughter (whom they later murdered). The emergency dispatcher couldn't be bothered with immediately sending police to chase the kidnappers/murders/rapists while the abducted little girl was still alive. First he had to take calls about a parking violation downtown and a complaint about harassing phone calls. When he got around to the kidnapping, he didn't issue an all-points bulletin but instead told just one officer to come back to the police station, not even mentioning that it was an emergency. Even more blazing negligence ensued, but suffice it to say that when the remnants of the family sued the city and the police, their case was summarily dismissed before going to trial. The state appeals court upheld the decision, claiming that the authorities have no duty to protect individuals.

Similarly, people in various states have been unable to successfully sue over the following situations:

- ☠ **when 911 systems have been shut down for maintenance**

- ☠ **when a known stalker kills someone**

- ☠ **when the police pull over but don't arrest a drunk driver who runs over someone later that night**

- ☠ **when a cop known to be violently unstable shoots a driver he pulled over for an inadequate muffler**

- ☠ **when authorities know in advance of a plan to commit murder but do nothing to stop it**

- ☠ **when parole boards free violent psychotics, including child rapist-murderers**

- ☠ **when felons escape from prison and kill someone**

- ☠ **when houses burn down because the fire department didn't respond promptly**

- ☠ **when children are beaten to death in foster homes**

A minority of states do offer a tiny bit of hope. In eighteen states, citizens have successfully sued over failure to protect, but even here the grounds have been very narrow. Usually, the police and the victim must have had a prior "special relationship" (for example, the authorities must have promised protection to this specific individual in the past). And, not surprisingly, many of these states have issued contradictory court rulings, or a conflict exists between state law and the rulings of the courts.

Don't look to Constitution for help. "In its landmark decision of *DeShaney v. Winnebago County Department of Social Services*," Stevens writes, "the US Supreme Court declared that the Constitution does not impose a duty on the state and local governments to protect the citizens from criminal harm."

All in all, as Stevens says, you'd be much better off owning a gun and learning how to use it. Even in those cases where you could successfully sue, this victory comes only after years (sometimes more than a decade) of wrestling with the justice system and only after you've been gravely injured or your loved one has been snuffed. ⏹

24
THE GOVERNMENT CAN TAKE YOUR HOUSE AND LAND, THEN SELL THEM TO PRIVATE CORPORATIONS

It's not an issue that gets much attention, but the government has the right to seize your house, business, and/or land, forcing you into the street. This mighty power, called "eminent domain," is enshrined in the US Constitution's Fifth Amendment: "…nor shall private property be taken for public use without just compensation." Every single state constitution also stipulates that a person whose property is taken must be justly compensated and that the property must be put to public use. This should mean that if your house is smack-dab in the middle of a proposed highway, the government can take it, pay you market value, and build the highway.

Whether or not this is a power the government should have is very much open to question, but what makes it worse is the abuse of this supposedly limited power. Across the country, local governments are stealing their citizens' property, then turning around and selling it to corporations for the construction of malls, condominiums, parking lots, racetracks, office complexes, factories, etc.

The Institute for Justice — the country's only nonprofit, public-interest law firm with a libertarian philosophy — spends a good deal of time protecting individuals and small businesses from greedy corporations and their partners in crime: bureaucrats armed with eminent domain. In 2003, it released a report on the use of "governmental condemnation" (another name for eminent domain) for private gain. No central data collection for this trend exists, and only one state (Connecticut) keeps statistics on it. Using court records, media accounts, and information from involved parties, the Institute found over *10,000* such abuses in 41 states from 1998 through 2002. Of these, the legal process had been initiated against 3,722 properties, and condemnation had been threatened against 6,560 properties. (Remember, this is condemnation solely for the benefit of private parties, not for so-called legitimate reasons of "public use.")

In one instance, the city of Hurst, Texas, condemned 127 homes so that a mall could expand. Most of the families moved under the pressure, but ten chose to stay and fight. The Institute writes:

A Texas trial judge refused to stay the condemnations while the suit was ongoing, so the residents lost their homes. Leonard Prohs had to move while his wife was in the hospital with brain cancer. She died only five days after their house was demolished. Phyllis Duval's husband also was in the hospital with cancer at the time they were required to move. He died one month after the demolition. Of the ten couples, three spouses died and four others suffered heart attacks during the dispute and litigation. In court, the owners presented evidence that the land surveyor who designed the roads for the mall had been told to change the path of one road to run through eight of the houses of the owners challenging the condemnations.

In another case, wanting to "redevelop" Main Street, the city of East Hartford, Connecticut, used eminent domain to threaten a bakery/deli that had been in that spot for 93 years, owned and operated by the same family during that whole time. Thus coerced, the family sold the business for $1.75 million, and the local landmark was destroyed. But the redevelopment fell through, so the lot now stands empty and the city is in debt.

The city of Cypress, California, wanted Costco to build a retail store on an 18-acre plot of land. Trouble was, the Cottonwood Christian Center already owned the land fair and square, and was planning to build a church on it. The city council used eminent domain to seize the land, saying that the new church would be a "public nuisance" and would "blight" the area (which is right beside a horse-racing track). The Christian Center got a federal injunction to stop the condemnation, and the city appealed this decision. To avoid further protracted legal nightmares, the church group consented to trade its land for another tract in the vicinity.

But all of this is small potatoes compared to what's going on in Riviera Beach, Florida:

City Council members voted unanimously to approve a $1.25 billion redevelopment plan with the authority to use eminent domain to condemn at least 1,700 houses and apartments and dislocate 5,100 people. The city will then take the property and sell the land to commercial yachting, shipping, and tourism companies.

If approved by the state, it will be one of the biggest eminent domain seizures in US history.

In 1795, the Supreme Court referred to eminent domain as "the despotic power." Over two centuries later, they continue to be proven right. ☐

25
THE SUPREME COURT HAS RULED THAT YOU'RE ALLOWED TO INGEST ANY DRUG, ESPECIALLY IF YOU'RE AN ADDICT

In the early 1920s, Dr. Linder was convicted of selling one morphine tablet and three cocaine tablets to a patient who was addicted to narcotics. The Supreme Court overturned the conviction, declaring that providing an addicted patient with a fairly small amount of drugs is an acceptable medical practice "when designed temporarily to alleviate an addict's pains." (*Linder v. United States*.)

In 1962, the Court heard the case of a man who had been sent to the clink under a California state law that made being an addict a criminal offense. Once again, the verdict was tossed out, with the Supremes saying that punishing an addict for being an addict is cruel and unusual and, thus, unconstitutional. (*Robinson v. California*.)

Six years later, the Supreme Court reaffirmed these principles in *Powell v. Texas*. A man who was arrested for being drunk in public said that, because he was an alcoholic, he couldn't help it. He invoked the *Robinson* decision as precedent. The Court upheld his conviction because it had been based on an action (being wasted in public), not on the general condition of his addiction to booze. Justice White supported this decision, yet for different reasons than the others. In his concurring opinion, he expanded *Robinson*:

If it cannot be a crime to have an irresistible compulsion to use narcotics,... I do

not see how it can constitutionally be a crime to yield to such a compulsion. Punishing an addict for using drugs convicts for addiction under a different name. Distinguishing between the two crimes is like forbidding criminal conviction for being sick with flu or epilepsy, but permitting punishment for running a fever or having a convulsion. Unless *Robinson* is to be abandoned, the use of narcotics by an addict must be beyond the reach of the criminal law. Similarly, the chronic alcoholic with an irresistible urge to consume alcohol should not be punishable for drinking or for being drunk.

Commenting on these cases, Superior Court Judge James P. Gray, an outspoken critic of drug prohibition, has recently written:

What difference is there between alcohol and any other dangerous and sometimes addictive drug? The primary difference is that one is legal while the others are not. And the US Supreme Court has said as much on at least two occasions, finding both in 1925 and 1962 that to punish a person for the disease of drug addiction violated the Constitution's prohibition on cruel and unusual punishment. If that is true, why do we continue to prosecute addicted people for taking these drugs, when it would be unconstitutional to prosecute them for their addiction?

Judge Gray gets right to the heart of the matter: "In effect, this 'forgotten precedent' says that one can only be constitutionally punishable for one's *conduct*, such as assaults, burglary, and driving under the influence, and not simply for what one puts into one's own body."

If only the Supreme Court and the rest of the justice/law-enforcement complex would apply these decisions, we'd be living in a saner society. ⌀

26
THE AGE OF CONSENT IN MOST OF THE US IS NOT EIGHTEEN

The accepted wisdom tells us that the age at which a person can legally consent to sex in the US is eighteen. Before this line of demarcation, a person is "jailbait" or "chicken." On their eighteenth birthday, they become "legal." But in the majority of states, this isn't the case.

It's up to each state to determine its own age of consent. Only fifteen states have put theirs at eighteen, with the rest going lower. Eight have set the magic point at the seventeenth birthday. The most popular age is sixteen, with 27 states and Washington DC setting the ability to sexually consent there. (Hawaii's age of consent had been fourteen until mid-2001, when it was bumped to sixteen.)

Of course, as with anything regarding the law, there are considerable shades of gray. For one thing, these laws don't apply if the lovers are married. The age of consent for marriage, especially with parental permission, is usually lower than the age of sexual consent.

The Constitution of the State of South Carolina says that females aged fourteen and up can consent to sex, but state law appears to set the age at sixteen.

In a lot of states, the age of the older partner is a consideration. For example, Tennessee doesn't consider sex with someone aged thirteen to seventeen to be statutory rape if the elder partner is less than four years older. So a nineteen-year-old could get it on with a sixteen-year-old without breaking the law. The most extreme example of this rule is in Delaware. If you're 30 or older, boffing a sixteen- or seventeen-year-old is a felony. But if you're 29 or younger, it's perfectly legal.

And let's not even get into Georgia's Public Law 16-6-18, which outlaws sex between anyone who isn't married, no matter what their ages or genders.

Then, of course, we have the laws regarding same-sex relations, which are completely illegal in fifteen or so states. In almost all of the others states, the age of consent for gay sex is the same as that for het-sex. Two exceptions are Nevada and New Hampshire, which both allow sixteen-year-olds to consent to a member of the opposite sex, but set the limit at eighteen for those who go the other way. Somewhat startlingly, even though New Mexico's age of consent for straights is seventeen, it's thirteen for gays and lesbians.

The situation around the world varies even more than within the US. The age of consent in the UK is sixteen, except in Northern Ireland, where it's a year older. Various territories in Australia set the age at sixteen or seventeen, and in Canada it's universally fourteen. The lowest age — in a few countries, such as Chile and Mexico — is twelve. Only one country is known to have set the age above eighteen — Tunisia, which feels that twenty is the acceptable age. ⌀

27
MOST SCIENTISTS DON'T READ
ALL OF THE ARTICLES THEY CITE

Every scientific discovery builds on what came before. Because of this, research papers are chock-full of references to previous papers, leading you to believe that those older studies actually have been read and digested and are now being expanded upon.

After noticing that a lot of citations with identical mistakes were showing up in various papers, two researchers at the University of California, Los Angeles, set out to study the problem. They looked at the way well-known, heavily-cited papers had been referenced in subsequent papers. Regarding an influential paper on crystals published in 1973, *New Scientist* explains:

They found it had been cited in other papers 4300 times, with 196 citations containing misprints in the volume, page or year. But despite the fact that a billion different versions of erroneous reference are possible, they counted only 45. The most popular mistake appeared 78 times.

Obviously, these pursuers of scientific truths hadn't actually read the original paper, but had just clipped the reference from another paper, a trick they probably learned in college and never stopped using. Of course, some of the scientists who got the citation right hadn't read the paper, either. In the final analysis:

The model shows that the distribution of misprinted citations of the 1973 paper

could only have arisen if 78 percent of all the citations, including the correct ones, were "cut and pasted" from a secondary source. Many of those who got it right were simply lucky. ♡

28
LOUIS PASTEUR SUPPRESSED EXPERIMENTS THAT DIDN'T SUPPORT HIS THEORIES

One of the greatest scientific duels in history occurred between those who believed that micro-organisms spontaneously generate in decaying organic matter and those who believed that the tiny creatures migrated there from the open air. From the late 1850s to the late 1870s, the eminent French chemist and microbiologist Louis Pasteur was locked in a death-match with proponents of spontaneous generation, especially Felix Pouchet.

The two camps performed experiments one after the other, both to prove their pet theory and to disprove the opponent's. As we know, Pasteur won the debate: The fact that microbes travel through the air is now accepted as a given, with spontaneous generation relegated to the slag heap of quaint, discarded scientific ideas. But Pasteur didn't win fair and square.

It turns out that some of Pasteur's experiments gave strong *support* to the notion that rotting organic matter produces life. Of course, years later those experiments were realized to have been flawed, but at the time they buttressed the position of Pasteur's enemies. So he kept them secret.

In his myth-busting book *Einstein's Luck*, medical and scientific historian John Waller writes: "In fact, throughout his feud with Pouchet, Pasteur described in his notebooks as 'successful' any experiment that seemed to disprove spontaneous generation and 'unsuccessful' any that violated his own private beliefs and experimental expectations."

When Pasteur's rivals performed experiments that supported their theory, Pasteur would not publicly replicate those studies. In one case, he simply refused to perform the experiment or even discuss it. In another, he hemmed and hawed so long that his rival gave up in exasperation. Waller notes: "Revealingly, although Pasteur publicly ascribed Bastian's results to sloppy methodology, in private he and his team took them rather more seriously. As Gerald Geison's study of Pasteur's notebooks has recently revealed, Pasteur's team spent several weeks secretly testing Bastian's findings and refining their own ideas on the distribution of germs in the environment."

Pasteur would rail at his rivals and even his mentor when he thought they weren't scrupulously following the scientific method, yet he had no qualms about trashing it when doing so suited his aims. Luckily for him, he was on the right side of the debate. And just why was he so cocksure that spontaneous generation was wrong? It had nothing to do with science. "In his notes he repeatedly insisted that only the Creator-God had ever exercised the power to convert the inanimate into the living," writes Waller. "The possibility that life could be created anew without man first discovering the secrets of the Creator was rejected without any attempt at scientific justification." ⌣

29
THE CREATOR OF THE GAIA HYPOTHESIS SUPPORTS NUCLEAR POWER

James Lovelock is one of the icons of the environmental movement. His idea that the Earth is a self-regulating, living organism (the GAIA hypothesis, first expounded in his 1979 book *GAIA: A New Look at Life on Earth*) provides the philosophical underpinning of environmentalism.

So it may be surprising that Lovelock is an enthusiastic supporter of nuclear energy, which he says has "great benefits and small risks." In the preface to the seemingly paradoxical book *Environmentalists for Nuclear Energy*, he writes: "I want to put it to you that the dangers of continuing to burn fossil fuels (oil, gas, coal) as our main energy source are far greater and they threaten not just individuals but civilization itself." The answer, he maintains, is the clean energy from nuke plants, which produce almost nothing that clogs up the atmosphere. As for what to do with all that radioactive waste, Lovelock has a shocking answer:

Natural ecosystems can stand levels of continuous radiation that would be intolerable in a city. The land around the failed Chernobyl power station was evacuated because its high radiation intensity made it unsafe for people, but this radioactive land is now rich in wildlife, much more so than neighboring populated areas. We call the ash from nuclear power nuclear waste and worry about its safe disposal. I wonder if instead we should use it as an incorruptible guardian of the beautiful places of the Earth. Who would dare cut down a forest in which was the storage place of nuclear ash?

Lovelock does admit that nuclear power is "potentially harmful to people," something that his brethren in the group Environmentalists for Nuclear Power often try to downplay. Truthfully, some of their points are good ones. More people have been killed by coal-mining than by nuclear power, even when you factor in the shorter time that nuclear power has existed. Most of the radiation we get zapped with comes from outer space (around two-thirds) and medical procedures (around a third), with only a smidgen from nuke plants.

Still, when you know about all the unpublicized accidents and near-meltdowns that have occurred, it's hard to be quite so blasé about the dangers. After all, the group's own literature says, "Nuclear energy is a very clean energy if it is well designed, well-built, well operated, and well managed." Trouble is, it's often none of those things. Design flaws, human error, corruption, incompetence, greed, and toothless oversight mean that in the real world, nuke plants often don't work as advertised. ♉

30
GENETICALLY-ENGINEERED HUMANS HAVE ALREADY BEEN BORN

The earthshaking news appeared in the medical journal *Human Reproduction* under the impenetrable headline: "Mitochondria in Human Offspring Derived From Ooplasmic Trans-plantation." The media put the story in heavy rotation for one day, then forgot about it. We all forgot about it.

But the fact remains that the world is now populated by dozens of children who were genetically engineered. It still sounds like science fiction, yet it's true.

In the first known application of germline gene therapy — in which an individual's genes are changed in a way that can be passed to offspring — doctors at a reproductive facility in New Jersey announced in March 2001 that nearly 30 healthy babies had been born with DNA from *three* people: dad, mom, and a second woman. Fifteen were the product of the fertility clinic, with the other fifteen or so coming from elsewhere.

The doctors believe that one cause for failure of women to conceive is that their ova contain old mitochondria (if you don't remember your high school biology class, mitochondria are the part of cells that provides energy). These sluggish eggs fail to attach to the uterine wall when fertilized. In order to soup them up, scientists injected them with mitochondria from a younger woman. Since mitochondria contain DNA, the kids have the genetic material of all three parties. The DNA from the "other woman" can even be passed down along the female line.

The big problem is that no one knows what effects this will have on the children or their progeny. In fact, this substitution of mitochondria hasn't been studied extensively on animals, never mind *homo sapiens*. The doctors reported that the kids are healthy, but they neglected to mention something crucial. Although the fertility clinic's technique resulted in fifteen babies, a total of seventeen fetuses had been created. One of them had been aborted, and the other miscarried. Why? Both of them had a rare genetic disorder, Turner syndrome, which only strikes females. Ordinarily, just one in 2,500 females is born with this condition, in which one of the X chromosomes is incomplete or totally missing. Yet two out of these seventeen fetuses had developed it

If we assume that nine of the fetuses were female (around 50 percent), then two of the nine female fetuses had this rare condition. Internal documents from the fertility clinic admit that this amazingly high rate might be due to the ooplasmic transfer.

Even before the revelation about Turner syndrome became known, many experts were appalled that the technique had been used. A responding article in *Human Reproduction* said, in a dry understatement: "Neither the safety nor efficacy of this method has been adequately investigated." Ruth Deech, chair of Britain's Human Fertilization and Embryology Authority, told the BBC: "There is a risk, not just to the baby, but to future generations which we really can't assess at the moment."

The number of children who have been born as a result of this technique is unknown. The original article gave the number as "nearly thirty," but this was in early 2001. At that time, at least two of the mutant children were already one year old.

Dr. Joseph Cummin, professor emeritus of biology at the University of Western Ontario, says that no further information about these 30 children has appeared in the medical literature or the media. As far as additional children born with two mommies and a daddy, Cummin says that a report out of Norway in 2003 indicated that ooplasmic transfer has been used to correct mitochondrial disease. He opines: "It seems likely that the transplants are going on, but very, very quietly in a regulatory vacuum, perhaps." ☐

31
THE INSURANCE INDUSTRY WANTS TO GENETICALLY TEST ALL POLICY HOLDERS

The insurance industry's party line is that it doesn't want to genetically test people who sign up for policies, a practice that would detect a predisposition to develop cancer, multiple sclerosis, and other diseases and disorders. The industry's internal documents tell a completely different story, though.

While researching *War Against the Weak* — his sweeping history of eugenics (and its successor, genetics) in the United States and Germany — Edwin Black found two reports written by insurers for insurers. "Genetic Information and Medical Expense" — published in June 2000 by the American Academy of Actuaries — intones that an inability to ask for genetic tests "would have a direct impact on premium rates, ultimately raising the cost of insurance for everyone."

A paper issued by the same group in spring 2002 goes further, envisioning a nightmare scenario in which the entire insurance industry collapses. The genetically impure can't be weeded out, thus meaning that more of them get covered. Because of this, the insurers have to pay out more benefits, which drives up premiums for everybody. This causes some people with perfect chromosomes to be unable to afford insurance, which means a higher percentage of the insured are chromosomally challenged. A downward spiral has started, with more benefits paid out, higher premiums charged, fewer healthy people covered, more benefits, higher premiums, fewer healthy people, etc. This, the report warns, "could eventually cause the insurers to become insolvent."

In the UK, insurance companies were widely screening applicants for genetic red flags until Parliament slapped a moratorium on the practice in 2001, allowing only one type of test to be used. British companies argue that they will go belly-up if the ban isn't lifted soon. Based on this alone, it's ridiculous for the US insurance industry to claim it isn't hoping to use these tests.

With the fate of the insurance racket supposedly hanging in the balance, how long can it be before genetic screening is mandatory when applying for health or life coverage? ⛝

32
SMOKING CAUSES PROBLEMS OTHER THAN LUNG CANCER AND HEART DISEASE

The fact that smoking causes lung disease and oral cancer isn't exactly news, and only tobacco industry executives would express (feigned) shock at being told. But cigarettes can lead to a whole slew of problems involving every system of your tar-filled body, and most people aren't aware of this.

The American Council on Science and Health's book *Cigarettes: What the Warning Label Doesn't Tell You* is the first comprehensive look at the medical evidence of all types of harm triggered by smoking. Referencing over 450 articles from medical journals and reviewed by

45 experts — mainly medical doctors and PhDs — if this book doesn't convince you to quit, nothing will.

Among some of the things that cancer sticks do:

☠️ Besides cancers of the head, neck, and lungs, ciggies are especially connected to cancers of the bladder, kidney, pancreas, and cervix. Newer evidence is adding leukemia and colorectal cancer to the list. Recent studies have also found at least a doubling of risk among smokers for cancers of the vulva and penis, as well as an eight-fold risk of anal cancer for men and a nine-fold risk for women.

☠️ Smoking trashes the ability of blood to flow, which results in a sixteen-fold greater risk of peripheral vascular disease. This triggers pain in the legs and arms, which often leads to an inability to walk and, in some instances, gangrene and/or amputation. Seventy-six percent of all cases are caused by smoking, more than for any other factor, including diabetes, obesity, and high blood pressure.

☠️ Smokers are at least two to three times more likely to develop the heartbreak of psoriasis. Even if that doesn't happen, they'll look old before their time. The American Council tells us, "Smokers in their 40s have facial wrinkles similar to those of nonsmokers in their 60s."

☠️ Smokers require more anesthesia for surgery, and they recover much more slowly. In fact, wounds of all kinds take longer to heal for smokers.

☠ Puffing helps to weaken bones, soft tissue, and spinal discs, causing all kinds of musculo-skeletal pain, more broken bones and ruptured discs, and longer healing time. "A non-smoker's leg heals an average of 80 percent faster than a smoker's broken leg."

☠ Smoking is heavily related to osteoporosis, the loss of bone mass, which results in brittle bones and more breaks.

☠ Cigarettes interfere with your ability to have kids. "The fertility rates of women who smoke are about 30 percent lower than those of nonsmokers." If you're an idiot who continues to smoke while you're expecting — even in this day and age, some people, including stars Catherine Zeta-Jones and Courtney Love, do this — you increase the risks of miscarriage, stillbirth, premature birth, low birth weight, underdevelopment, and cleft pallet. If your child is able to survive outside the womb, it will have a heavily elevated risk of crib death (SIDS), allergies, and intellectual impairment.

☠ Smoking also does a serious number on sperm, resulting in more deformed cells, less ability of them to swim, smaller loads, and a drastic decrease in overall number of the little fellas. The larger population of misshapen sperm probably increases the risk of miscarriages and birth defects, so even if mommy doesn't smoke, daddy could still cause problems. What's more, because smoking hurts blood flow, male smokers are at least twice as likely to be unable to get it up.

☠ Besides shutting down blood flow to the little head, smoking interferes with the blood going to the big head in both sexes. This causes one quarter of all strokes. It also makes these strokes more likely to occur earlier in life and more likely to be fatal.

☠ "Depression — whether viewed as a trait, a symptom or a diagnosable disorder — is over-represented among smokers." Unfortunately, it's unclear how the two are related. Does smoking cause depression, or does depression lead to smoking? Or, most likely, do the two feed on each other in a vicious cycle?

☠ "Smokers experience sudden hearing loss an average of 16 years earlier than do never smokers."

☠ Smokers and former smokers have an increased risk of developing cataracts, abnormal eye movements, inflammation of the optic nerve, permanent blindness from lack of blood flow, and the most severe form of macular degeneration.

☠ Lighting up increases plaque, gum disease, and tooth loss.

☠ It also makes it likelier that you'll develop diabetes, stomach ulcers, colon polyps, and Crohn's disease.

☠ Smoking trashes the immune system in myriad ways, with the overall result being that you're more susceptible to disease and allergies.

☠ And let's not forget that second-hand smoke has horrible effects on the estimated 42 percent of toddlers and infants who are forced to inhale it in their homes:

According to the Environmental Protection Agency (EPA), children's "passive smoking," as it is called, results in hundreds of thousands of cases of bronchitis, pneumonia, ear infections, and worsened asthma. Worse yet, the Centers for Disease Control and Prevention estimates that 702 children younger than one year die each year as a result of sudden infant death syndrome (SIDS), worsened asthma and serious respiratory infections.

It's very surprising to note that smoking can have a few health *benefits*. Because they zap women's estrogen levels, cigarettes can lead to less endometriosis and other conditions related to the hormone. Smoking also decreases the risk of developing osteoarthritis in the knees, perhaps because the pliability of thin bones takes some pressure off of the cartilage. And because it jacks up dopamine levels, it helps ward off Parkinson's disease. Of course, these benefits seem to be side effects of the hazards of smoking, so the trade-off hardly seems worth it. ▯

33
HERDS OF MILK-PRODUCING COWS ARE RIFE WITH BOVINE LEUKEMIA VIRUS

Bovine leukemia virus is a cancer-causing microbe in cattle. Just how many cows have it? The US Department of Agriculture reports that nationwide, *89 percent* of herds contain cows with BLV. The most infected region is the Southeast, where 99 percent of herds have the tumor-causing bug. In some herds across the country, almost every single animal is infected. A 1980 study across Canada uncovered a lower but none-too-reassuring rate of 40 percent.

BLV is transmitted through milk. Since the milk from all cows in a herd is mixed before processing, if even a single cow is infected, all milk from that herd will have BLV swimming in it. Citing an article in *Science*, oncologist Robert Kradjian, MD, warns that 90 to 95 percent of milk starts out tainted. Of course, pasteurization — when done the right way — kills BLV, but the process isn't perfect. And if you drink raw milk, odds are you're gulping down bovine leukemia virus.

Between dairy cows and their cousins that are used for meat (who tend to be infected at lower rates), it appears that a whole lot of BLV is getting inside us. A 2001 study in *Breast Cancer Research* detected antibodies to the bovine leukemia virus in blood samples from 77 out of 100 volunteers. Furthermore, BLV showed up more often in breast tissue from women with breast cancer than in the tissue from healthy women. Several medical studies have found positive correlations between higher intake of milk/beef and increased incidence of leukemia or lymphoma in humans, although other studies haven't found a correlation.

No hard evidence has yet linked BLV to diseases in humans, but do you feel comfortable knowing that cow cancer cells are in your body? ⏻

34
MOST DOCTORS DON'T KNOW THE RADIATION LEVEL OF CAT SCANS

Using extended doses of encircling X-rays, CAT scans give a detailed look inside your body, revealing not only bones but soft tissue and blood vessels, as well. According to the health site Imaginis.com, over 70,000 places around the world offer CAT scans to detect and diagnose tumors, heart disease, osteoporosis, blood clots, spinal fractures, nerve damage, and lots of other problems. Because it can uncover so much, its use has become widespread and continues to rise. In fact, healthy people are getting scans just to see if anything might be wrong, kind of like a routine check-up.

The downside, and it's a doozy, is that a CAT scan jolts you with *100 to 250 times* the dose of radiation that you get from a chest X-ray. What's even more alarming is that most doctors apparently don't know this.

An emergency physician from the Yale School of Medicine surveyed 45 of his colleagues about the pros and cons of CAT scans. A mere nine of them said that they tell patients about the radiation. This might be just as well, in a weird way, since most of them had absolutely no clue about how much radiation CAT scans give off. When asked to compare the blast from a chest X-ray to the blast from a CAT scan, only 22 percent of the docs got it right. As for the other three-quarters, *The Medical Post* relates:

Three of the doctors said the dose was either less than or equal to a chest X-ray.

Twenty (44%) of the doctors said the dose was greater than a chest X-ray, but less than 10 times the dose. Just over one-fifth of the doctors (22%) said the radiation dose from a CT was more than 10 times that of an X-ray but less than 100 times the dose.

Only ten of them knew that a single CAT scan equals 100 to 250 chest X-rays, while two thought that the scans were even worse than that.

Feel free to give your doc a pop quiz during your next office visit. ロ

35
MEDICATION ERRORS KILL THOUSANDS EACH YEAR

Next time you get a prescription filled, look at the label very carefully. Getting the wrong drug or the wrong dosage kills hundreds or thousands of people each year, with many times that number getting injured.

Renegade health reporter Nicholas Regush — a self-imposed exile from ABC News — provides a long list of specific problems:

Poor handwriting. Verbal orders. Ambiguous orders. Prescribing errors. Failure to write orders. Unapproved uses. When the order is not modified or cancelled. Look-alike and sound-alike drug names. Dangerous abbreviations. Faulty drug

distribution systems in hospital. Failure to read the label or poor labeling. Lack of knowledge about drugs. Lack of knowledge concerning proper dose. Lack of knowledge concerning route of administration. Ad nauseam.

After pouring over death certificates, sociology professor David Philips — an expert in mortality statistics — determined that drug errors kill 7,000 people each year in the US. His study was published in *The Lancet*, probably the most prestigious medical journal in the world. The Institute of Medicine, a branch of the National Academies of Science, also estimated 7,000. Interestingly, the Food and Drug Administration published the lowball figure of 365 annually (one per day). But even the FDA admits that such bungling injures *1.3 million* people each year.

New York *Newsday* cited several specific cases, such as: "In 1995, a Texas doctor wrote an illegible prescription causing the patient to receive not only the wrong medication, but at eight times the drug's usually recommended strength. The patient, Ramon Vasquez, died. In 1999, a court ordered the doctor and pharmacy to pay the patient's family a total of $450,000, the largest amount ever awarded in an illegible prescription case."

Besides doctors' indecipherable chicken scratch, similar-sounding drug names are another big culprit. Pharmaceutical companies have even started warning medical professionals to be careful with the cookie-cutter names of their products. In a typical example, Celebrex, Cerebyx, Celexa, and Zyprexa sometimes get confused. (Respectively, they're used to treat arthritis, seizures, depression, and psychosis.) According to WebMD: "Bruce Lambert, an assistant professor of pharmacy administration at the University of Illinois at Chicago, says there are 100,000 potential pairings of drug names that could be confused." ⌷

36
PRESCRIPTION DRUGS KILL OVER 100,000 ANNUALLY

Even higher than the number of people who die from medication errors is the number of people who die from medication, period. Even when a prescription drug is dispensed properly, there's no guarantee it won't end up killing you.

A remarkable study in the *Journal of the American Medical Association* revealed that prescription drugs kill around 106,000 people in the US every year, which ranks prescription drugs as the fourth leading cause of death. Furthermore, each years sees 2,216,000 *serious* adverse drug reactions (defined as "those that required hospitalization, were permanently disabling, or resulted in death").

The authors of this 1998 study performed a meta-analysis on 39 previous studies covering 32 years. They factored out such things as medication errors, abuse of prescription drugs, and adverse reactions not considered serious. Plus, the study involved only people who had either been hospitalized due to drug reactions or who experienced reactions while in the hospital. People who died immediately (and, thus, never went to the hospital) and those whose deaths weren't realized to be due to prescription drugs were not included, so the true figure is probably higher.

Four years later, another study in the *JAMA* warned:

Patient exposure to new drugs with unknown toxic effects may be extensive. Nearly 20 million patients in the United States took at least 1 of the 5 drugs withdrawn from the market between September 1997 and September 1998. Three of these 5 drugs were new, having been on the market for less than 2 years. Seven drugs approved since 1993 and subsequently withdrawn from the market have been reported as possibly contributing to 1002 deaths.

Examining warnings added to drug labels through the years, the study's authors found that of the new chemical entities approved from 1975 to 1999, 10 percent "acquired a new black box warning or were withdrawn from the market" by 2000. Using some kind of high-falutin' statistical process, they estimate that the "probability of a new drug acquiring black box warnings or being withdrawn from the market over 25 years was 20%."

A statement released by one of the study's coauthors — Sidney Wolfe, MD, Director of Public Citizen's Health Studies Group — warned:

In 1997, 39 new drugs were approved by the FDA. As of now [May 2002], five of them (Rezulin, Posicor, Duract, Raxar and Baycol) have been taken off the market and an additional two (Trovan, an antibiotic and Orgaran, an anticoagulant) have had new box warnings. Thus, seven drugs approved that year (18% of the 39 drugs approved) have already been withdrawn or had a black box warning in just four years after approval. Based on our study, 20% of drugs will be withdrawn or have a

black box warning within 25 years of coming on the market. The drugs approved in 1997 have already almost "achieved" this in only four years — with 21 years to go.

How does this happen? Before the FDA approves a new drug, it must undergo clinical trials. These trials aren't performed by the FDA, though — they're done by the drug companies themselves. These trials often use relatively few patients, and they usually select patients most likely to react well to the drug. On top of that, the trials are often for a short period of time (weeks), even though real-world users may be on a drug for months or years at a time. Dr. Wolfe points out that even when adverse effects show up during clinical trials, the drugs are sometimes released anyway, and they end up being taken off the market because of those same adverse effects.

Postmarketing reporting of adverse effects isn't much better. The FDA runs a program to collect reports of problems with drugs, but compliance is voluntary. The generally accepted estimate in the medical community is that a scant 10 percent of individual instances of adverse effects are reported to the FDA, which would mean that the problem is ten times worse than we currently believe.

Drugs aren't released when they've been proven safe; they're released when enough FDA bureaucrats — many of whom have worked for the pharmaceutical companies or will work for them in the future — can be convinced that it's kinda safe. Basically, the use of prescription drugs by the general public can be seen as widespread, long-term clinical trials to determine their *true* safety.

We are all guinea pigs. ▯

37
WORK KILLS MORE PEOPLE THAN WAR

The United Nations' International Labor Organization has revealed some horrifying stats:

The ILO estimates that approximately two million workers lose their lives annually due to occupational injuries and illnesses, with accidents causing at least 350,000 deaths a year. For every fatal accident, there are an estimated 1,000 non-fatal injuries, many of which result in lost earnings, permanent disability and poverty. The death toll at work, much of which is attributable to unsafe working practices, is the equivalent of 5,000 workers dying each day, three persons every minute.

This is more than double the figure for deaths from warfare (650,000 deaths per year). According to the ILO's SafeWork programme, work kills more people than alcohol and drugs together and the resulting loss in Gross Domestic Product is 20 times greater than all official development assistance to the developing countries.

Each year, 6,570 US workers die because of injuries at work, while 60,225 meet their maker due to occupational diseases. (Meanwhile, 13.2 million get hurt, and 1.1 million develop illnesses that don't kill them.) On an average day, two or three workers are fatally shot, two fall to their deaths, one is killed after being smashed by a vehicle, and one is electrocuted. Each year, around 30 workers die of heat stroke, and another 30 expire from carbon monoxide.

Although blue collar workers face a lot of the most obvious dangers, those slaving in offices or stores must contend with toxic air, workplace violence, driving accidents, and (especially for the health-care workers) transmissible diseases. The Occupational Safety and Health Administration warns that poisonous indoor air in nonindustrial workplaces causes "[t]housands of heart disease deaths [and] hundreds of lung cancer deaths" each year.

But hey, everybody has to go sometime, right? And since we spend so much of our lives in the workplace, it's only logical that a lot of deaths happen — or at least are set into motion — on the job. This explanation certainly is true to an extent, but it doesn't excuse all such deaths. The International Labor Organization says that half of workplace fatalities are avoidable. In *A Job to Die For*, Lisa Cullen writes:

In the workplace, few real accidents occur because the surroundings and operations are known; therefore, hazards can be identified. When harm from those hazards can be foreseen, accidents can be prevented….

Most jobs have expected, known hazards. Working in and near excavations, for example, poses the obvious risks of death or injury from cave-in…. When trenches or excavations collapse because soil was piled right up to the edge, there is little room to claim it was an accident. ⌗

38
THE SUICIDE RATE IS HIGHEST AMONG THE ELDERLY

If you judge by the media and the public education programs, you might be inclined to think that teenagers and young adults (aged 15 to 24) are the age group most likely to kill themselves. Actually, they have the second-*lowest* rate of suicide. (The absolute lowest rate is among kids aged 5 to 14; children younger than that are apparently deemed incapable of consciously choosing to end their lives.) It is the elderly, by far, who have the highest rate of suicide.

In the US, of every 100,000 people aged 75 to 79, 16.5 kill themselves. For those 80 and over, the rate is 19.43. This compares to a rate of 8.15 per 100,000 for people between the ages of 15 and 19, and 12.84 for people aged 20 to 24.

As with every age group, men are far more likely to kill themselves, but among the elderly this trend reaches extreme proportions. Of people 65 and older, men comprise a staggering 84 percent of suicides.

Because men commit the vast majority of *hara-kiri* among old people, looking at these male suicide rates makes for extremely depressing reading. For guys aged 75 to 79, the suicide rate is 34.26 per 100,000. In the 80 to 84 group, men's suicide rate is 44.12. When you look at men 85 and older, the suicide rate is a heart-breaking 54.52. Compare this to the suicide rate for dudes in their mid to late teens: 13.22 per 100,000.

It is true that suicide ranks as the second or third most common cause of death in young people (depending on age group), while it is number 15 and under for various groups of the elderly. Still, the suicide rate among the young is equal to their proportion of the population, while the elderly are way overrepresented as a group. And old people are cut down by a great many diseases and disorders virtually unknown to the young, which naturally pushes suicide down in the rankings.

The reasons why this suicide epidemic is ignored are highly speculative and would be too lengthy to get into here. However, we can rule out one seemingly likely explanation — suicide among the aged is invisible because they usually O.D. on prescription drugs or kill themselves in other ways that could easily be mistaken for natural death in someone of advanced years. This doesn't wash, primarily because guns are the most common method of dispatch. Of suicides over 65, men used a gun 79.5 percent of the time, while women shot themselves 37 percent of the time. It's hard to mistake that for natural causes.

The sky-high suicide rate among the elderly applies to the entire world, not just the US. Plotted in a graph, suicide rates by age group around the globe gently curve upward as age increases. When the graph reaches the final age group, the line suddenly spikes, especially for men. Worldwide, men 75 and over have a suicide rate of 55.7 per 100,000, while women in the same age group have a rate of 18.8. This rate for old men is almost three times the global rate for guys aged 15 to 24, while the rate for old women is well over three times the rate for young gals in that age group. ⌧

39
FOR LOW-RISK PEOPLE, A POSITIVE RESULT FROM AN HIV TEST IS WRONG HALF THE TIME

Although a lot of progress has been made in improving the length and quality of life for people with AIDS, getting a positive result from an HIV test must still rank as one of the worst pieces of news a person can get. It's not uncommon for people to kill themselves right after hearing the results, and those who don't commit suicide surely go through all kinds of mental anguish. But the accuracy of these tests is lower than generally believed. In fact, if you test positive but you're not a member of a high-risk group (such as non-monogamous gay men and intravenous drug users), the odds are 50-50 that you actually have the virus.

To be declared HIV-positive, your blood goes through three tests — two ELISA tests and one more sensitive and costly Western Blot test. Makers of the tests trumpet a 99.99 percent accuracy rate when all three are used. Many AIDS counselors even tell people that the tests *never* give a false positive (that is, the tests don't indicate that someone is HIV-positive when he or she really isn't). The test manufacturers' claim is misleading, and the counselors' claim is flat-out BS. Cognitive scientist Gerd Gigerenzer — who specializes in risk and uncertainty — explains the reality in plain English:

Imagine 10,000 men who are not in any known risk category. One is infected (base rate) and will test positive with practical certainty (sensitivity). Of the 9,999 men who are not infected, another one will also test positive (false positive rate). So we can expect that two men will test positive.

Out of these two men, only one actually carries the virus. So, if you're a low-risk man who tests positive, the chances are even — the same as a coin flip — that the result is right. It's highly advisable that you take the tests again (and again). The results are even less reliable for women in low-risk groups, since they have a still lower rate of HIV.

Of course, this doesn't apply to an HIV-negative result. If you test negative, the odds are overwhelmingly good (9,998 out of 9,999) that this is correct. It also doesn't hold for people in high-risk categories. For example, if we accept the estimate that 1.5 percent of gay men are HIV-positive, this means that out of every 10,000, an average of 150 are infected. An HIV test will almost surely pick up on all 150, and out of the remaining 9,850 uninfected men, one will incorrectly be labeled positive. This means that only one out of 151 gay men will be falsely diagnosed as having HIV. A false positive is thus still possible but much more unlikely. ♡

40
DNA MATCHING IS NOT INFALLIBLE

Speaking of tests that aren't all they're cracked up to be, let's look at DNA testing. This is supposed to be the absolute silver bullet of criminal justice, an incontrovertible way to pin guilt on someone. After all, the chances of a mismatch are one in a billion, a quadrillion, a jillion! Some experts have testified under oath that a false match is literally impossible.

Not quite. As he did with HIV testing, risk scholar Gerd Gigerenzer of the Max Planck Institute punches a hole in the matching of genetic material:

In the first blind test reported in the literature, three major commercial laboratories were each sent 50 DNA samples. Two of the three declared one false match; in a second test one year later, one of the same three laboratories declared a false match. From external tests conducted by the California Association of Crime Laboratory Directors, the Collaborative Testing Services, and other agencies, the psychologist Jonathan Koehler and his colleagues estimated the false positive rate of DNA fingerprinting to be on the order of 1 in 100. Cellmark Diagnostics, one of the laboratories that found matches between O.J. Simpson's DNA and DNA extracted from a recovered blood stain at the murder scene, reported its own false positive rate to the Simpson defense as roughly 1 in 200.

It gets even worse. In 1999, the College of American Pathologists performed its own secret tests of 135 labs. Each lab was sent a DNA sample from the "victim," some semen from the "suspect," and a fake vaginal swab containing DNA from both parties. They were also sent a strand of the "victim's" hair. The object was to see how many of the labs would make the matches (ie, match the two sperm samples of the man, and match the hair and DNA sample of the woman). But something unexpected happened: Three of the labs reported that the DNA from the suspect matched the victim's DNA! Obviously, they had mixed up the samples. Only fourteen labs tested the hair, but out of those, one screwed it up by declaring a match to the "suspect."

These kind of switches don't happen only during artificial situations designed to gauge a lab's accuracy (which are usually performed under ideal conditions). During a 1995 rape trial, a lab reversed the labels on the DNA samples from the victim and the defendant. Their testing then revealed a match between the defendant's alleged DNA (which was actually the victim's) and the

DNA on the vaginal swab, which didn't contain any semen from the rapist. Luckily, this boneheaded move was caught during the trial, but not everyone is so lucky.

The *Journal of Forensic Science* has reported an error that was discovered only after an innocent man had been convicted of raping an 11-year-old girl and sentenced to prison, where he was undoubtedly brutalized in ways that would give you nightmares for the rest of your life, were you to hear them described in detail. After four years, he was released because the lab hadn't completely separated the real rapist's DNA (extracted from his semen) from the victim's DNA. When the two were swirled together, they somehow matched that of the poor bastard whose eleven alibi witnesses failed to sway the jury. But when the semen DNA was checked properly, it was beyond doubt that a match didn't exist.

While most false matches are the result of human error, other factors do come into play. Some testing techniques are more definitive than others. In the case of one innocent man — Josiah Sutton, found guilty of rape based primarily on DNA evidence — criminology professor William C. Thompson said: "If police picked any two black men off the street, the chances that one of them would have a DNA profile that 'matched' the semen sample as well as Sutton's profile is better than one in eight." Also, we mustn't forget about corruption. In some known cases, DNA analysts have misrepresented (ie, lied about) their findings in order to obtain convictions. ⊐

41
AN FBI EXPERT TESTIFIED THAT LIE DETECTORS ARE WORTHLESS FOR SECURITY SCREENING

Now let's turn our attention to the last member of our trifecta of defective tests — the polygraph, more commonly referred to as the lie detector. Invented by the same person who created Wonder Woman and her golden lasso that makes you tell the truth (I'm not kidding), the polygraph is said to detect deception based on subtle bodily signals, such as pulse rate and sweatiness. Its proponents like to claim that it has a success rate of 90 percent or more. This is pure hogwash. While the evidence against lie detectors is way too voluminous to get into here, it will be very instructive to look at a statement from Dr. Drew Richardson. Richardson is a scientist who was an FBI agent for 25 years; in the late 1980s and early 1990s, he dealt with polygraphs.

In fall 1997, a Senate Judiciary subcommittee held hearings regarding the FBI Crime Lab. Richardson gave scorching testimony about polygraphs. Referring specifically to the practice of using lie detectors to question people in sensitive positions, he said under oath:

It is completely without any theoretical foundation and has absolutely no validity. Although there is disagreement amongst scientists about the use of polygraph testing in criminal matters, there is almost universal agreement that polygraph screening is completely invalid and should be stopped. As one of my colleagues frequently says, the diagnostic value of this type of testing is no more than that of astrology or tea-leaf reading.

If this test had any validity (which it does not), both my own experience, and published scientific research has proven, that anyone can be taught to beat this type of polygraph exam in a few minutes.

Because of the nature of this type of examination, it would normally be expected to produce large numbers of false positive results (falsely accusing an examinee of lying about some issue). As a result of the great consequences of doing this with large numbers of law enforcement and intelligence community officers, the test has now been manipulated to reduce false positive results, but consequently has no power to detect deception in espionage and other national security matters. Thus, I believe that there is virtually no probability of catching a spy with the use of polygraph screening techniques. I think a careful examination of the Aldrich Ames case will reveal that any shortcomings in the use of the polygraph were not simply errors on the part of the polygraph examiners involved, and would not have been eliminated if FBI instead of CIA polygraphers had conducted these examinations. Instead I believe this is largely a reflection of the complete lack of validity of this methodology. To the extent that we place any confidence in the results of polygraph screening, and as a consequence shortchange traditional security vetting techniques, I think our national security is severely jeopardized.

After he ripped polygraphs a new one, the FBI silenced Richardson, refusing to let him speak publicly about the subject again. ↻

42
THE BAYER COMPANY MADE HEROIN

Aspirin isn't the only "wonder drug that works wonders" that Bayer made. The German pharmaceutical giant also introduced heroin to the world.

The company was looking for a cough suppressant that didn't have problematic side effects, mainly addiction, like morphine and codeine. And if it could relieve pain better than morphine, that was a welcome bonus.

When one of Bayer's chemists approached the head of the pharmacological lab with ASA — to be sold under the name "aspirin" — he was waved away. The boss was more interested in something else the chemists had cooked up — diacetyl-morphine. (This narcotic had been created in 1874 by a British chemist, who had never done anything with it.)

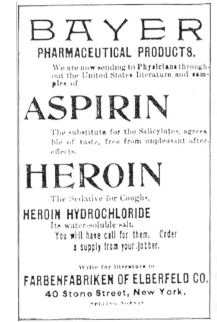

Using the tradename "Heroin" — because early testers said it made them feel *heroisch* (heroic) — Bayer sold this popular drug by the truckload starting in 1898. Free samples were sent to thousands of doctors; studies appeared in medical journals. The *Sunday Times* of London noted: "By 1899, Bayer was producing about a ton of heroin a year, and exporting the drug to 23 countries," including the US. Medicines containing smack were available over-the-counter at drug stores, just as aspirin is today. The American Medical Association gave heroin its stamp of approval in 1907.

But reports of addiction, which had already started appearing in 1899, turned into a torrent after several years. Bayer had wisely released aspirin the year after heroin, and this new non-addictive painkiller and anti-inflammatory was well on its way to becoming the most popular drug ever. In 1913, Bayer got out of the heroin business.

Not that the company has kept its nose clean since then:

A division of the pharmaceutical company Bayer sold millions of dollars of blood-clotting medicine for hemophiliacs — medicine that carried a high risk of transmitting AIDS — to Asia and Latin America in the mid-1980s while selling a new, safer product in the West, according to documents obtained by *The New York Times*…. [I]n Hong Kong and Taiwan alone, more than 100 hemophiliacs got HIV after using Cutter's old medicine, according to records and interviews. Many have since died. ⌣

43
LSD HAS BEEN USED SUCCESSFULLY IN PSYCHIATRIC THERAPY

Given the demonization of the psychedelic drug LSD, it may seem inconceivable that mainstream psychiatrists were giving it to patients during sessions. Yet for at least 20 years, that's exactly what happened.

Created in 1938, LSD was first suggested as a tool in psychotherapy in 1949. The following year saw the first studies in medical/psychiatric journals. By 1970, hundreds of articles on the uses of LSD in therapy had appeared in the *Journal of the American Medical Association*, the *Journal of Psychology*, the *Archives of General Psychiatry*, the *Quarterly Journal of Studies of Alcoholism*, many non-English-language journals, and elsewhere.

Psychiatric and psychotherapeutic conferences had segments devoted to LSD, and two professional organizations were formed for this specialty, one in Europe and the other in North America. International symposia were held in Princeton, London, Amsterdam, and other locations. From 1950 to 1965, LSD was given in conjunction with therapy to an estimated 40,000 people worldwide.

In his definitive book on the subject, *LSD Psychotherapy*, transpersonal psychotherapist Stanislav Grof, MD, explains what makes LSD such a good aid to headshrinking:

...LSD and other psychedelics function more or less as nonspecific catalysts and

amplifiers of the psyche.... In the dosages used in human experimentation, the classical psychedelics, such as LSD, psilocybin, and mescaline, do not have any specific pharmacological effects. They increase the energetic niveau in the psyche and the body which leads to manifestation of otherwise latent psychological processes.

The content and nature of the experiences that these substances induce are thus not artificial products of their pharmacological interaction with the brain ("toxic psychoses"), but authentic expressions of the psyche revealing its functioning on levels not ordinarily available for observation and study. A person who has taken LSD does not have an "LSD experience," but takes a journey into deep recesses of his or her own psyche.

When used as a tool during full-scale therapy, Grof says, "the potential of LSD seems to be extraordinary and unique. The ability of LSD to deepen, intensify and accelerate the psychotherapeutic process is incomparably greater than that of any other drug used as an adjunct to psychotherapy, with the exception perhaps of some other members of the psychedelic group."

Due to bad trips experienced by casual users, not to mention anti-drug hysteria in general, LSD was outlawed in the US in 1970. The Drug Enforcement Agency declares: "Scientific study of LSD ceased circa 1980 as research funding declined."

What the DEA fails to mention is that medical and psychiatric research is currently happening, albeit quietly. Few researchers have the resources and patience to jump through the umpteen hoops required to test psychedelics on people, but a few experiments using LSD, ecstasy, DMT ketamine, peyote, and other such substances are happening in North America and Europe Universities engaged in this research include Harvard, Duke, Johns Hopkins, University College London, and the University of Zurich.

We're presently in the dark ages of such research, but at least the light hasn't gone out entirely

44
CARL SAGAN WAS AN AVID POT-SMOKER

When you're talking about scientists who achieved rock-star status in the second half of the twentieth century, the late astronomer and biologist Carl Sagan is right up there with Stephen Hawking. His *Cosmos* (1980) is one of the most popular science books ever written, planting itself on the *New York Times* bestseller list for 70 weeks and staying perpetually in print ever since. It was a companion for the PBS television series of the same name, which — along with numerous *Tonight Show* appearances — introduced Sagan and his emphatically stated phrase "billions and billions" into pop culture. His sole novel, *Contact*, was turned into a love-it-or-hate-it movie starring Jodie Foster as an erstwhile scientist searching for extraterrestrial life, with Matthew McConaughey as a New Age flake who, inevitably, makes his own form of contact with her.

Besides his pop-culture credentials, Sagan was pals with numerous legendary Nobel Prize-winners while still in college, picked up a Pulitzer Prize for his book *Dragons of Eden*, and consulted for NASA, MIT, Cornell, and RAND. He designed the human race's postcards to any aliens that might be out there — the plaque onboard the *Pioneer* space probes and the record on the *Voyager* probes.

So it might come as a bit of a surprise that Sagan was an avid smoker of marijuana. Some might even call him a pothead.

In his definitive biography of the celebrity scientist, Keay Davidson reveals that Sagan started toking regularly in the early 1960s and that *Dragons of Eden* — which won the Pulitzer — "was obviously written under the inspiration of marijuana." Davidson says of Sagan:

He believed the drug enhanced his creativity and insights. His closest friend of three decades, Harvard psychiatry professor Dr. Lester Grinspoon, a leading advocate of the decriminalization of marijuana, recalls an incident in the 1980s when one of his California admirers mailed him, unsolicited, some unusually high-quality pot. Grinspoon shared the joints with Sagan and his wife, Anne Druyan. Afterward, Sagan said, "Lester, I know you've only got one left, but could I have it? I've got serious work to do tomorrow and I could really use it."

Perhaps letting Sagan bogart the pot was Grinspoon's way of returning a favor, since Sagan had contributed an essay to *Marihuana Reconsidered*, Grinspoon's classic 1971 book on the benefits and low risks of reefer. For almost three decades, the author of this ode to Mary Jane was anonymous, but in 1999 Grinspoon revealed that "Mr. X" was Sagan.

In the essay, Sagan wrote that weed increased his appreciation of art, music, food, sex, and childhood memories, and gave him insights into scientific and social matters:

I can remember one occasion, taking a shower with my wife while high, in which I had an idea on the origins and invalidities of racism in terms of Gaussian distribution curves. It was a point obvious [sic] in a way, but rarely talked about. I drew curves in soap on the shower wall, and went to write the idea down. One idea led to another, and at the end of about an hour of extremely hard work I found I had written eleven short essays on a wide range of social, political, philosophical, and human biological topics.... I have used them in university commencement addresses, public lectures, and in my books.

The staunchly atheistic/humanistic Sagan comes perilously close to mysticism in some passages:

I do not consider myself a religious person in the usual sense, but there is a religious aspect to some highs. The heightened sensitivity in all areas gives me a feeling of communion with my surroundings, both animate and inanimate. Sometimes a kind of existential perception of the absurd comes over me and I see with awful certainty the hypocrisies and posturing of myself and my fellow

men. And at other times, there is a different sense of the absurd, a playful and whimsical awareness....

I am convinced that there are genuine and valid levels of perception available with cannabis (and probably with other drugs) which are, through the defects of our society and our educational system, unavailable to us without such drugs. Such a remark applies not only to self-awareness and to intellectual pursuits, but also to perceptions of real people, a vastly enhanced sensitivity to facial expression, intonations, and choice of words which sometimes yields a rapport so close it's as if two people are reading each other's minds. ♀

45
ONE OF THE HEROES OF *BLACK HAWK DOWN* IS A CONVICTED CHILD MOLESTER

The movie *Black Hawk Down* was one of the biggest box office draws of 2001, and it earned its director, Ridley Scott, an Oscar nomination. (He didn't win, but the movie got two Academy Awards for editing and sound.) Based on Mark Bowden's nonfiction book of the same title, it concerns the disastrous raid of Mogadishu, Somalia, by US elite soldiers in 1993.

One of these Special Forces soldiers underwent a name-change as he moved from the printed page to the big screen. Ranger John "Stebby" Stebbins became Ranger Danny Grimes when played by Scottish heartthrob Ewan McGregor. Why? Because in 2000, Stebbins was court-martialed and sent to the stockade for rape and sodomy of a child under twelve.

This decidedly unheroic turn of events was confirmed by the Army, the Fort Leavenworth military prison (Stebby's home for the next 30 years), and *Black Hawk Down*'s author. Bowden told the *New York Post* that the Army asked him to change Stebbins' name in the screenplay in order to avoid embarrassing the military.

In an email to the newspaper, Stebby's ex-wife, Nora Stebbins, wrote: "They are going to make millions off this film in which my ex-husband is portrayed as an All-American hero when the truth is he is not." ▢

46
THE AUTO INDUSTRY SAYS THAT SUV DRIVERS ARE SELFISH AND INSECURE

People who tool around in hulking, big-ass sport utility vehicles have been getting dissed a lot lately, but no one has raked them over the coals like the people who sold them the SUVs in the first place. The multibillion-dollar auto industry does extensive research into its customers, and lately that research has focused quite a bit on the people who buy SUVs.

Investigative reporter Keith Bradsher of the *New York Times* has looked into the SUV phenomenon for years. He's read marketing reports meant only to be seen within the industry, he's interviewed marketing executives from the car companies and from outside research firms,

The industry has come to some unflattering conclusions about the people who buy its SUVs. As summarized by Bradsher:

They tend to be people who are insecure and vain. They are frequently nervous about their marriages and uncomfortable about parenthood. They often lack confidence in their driving skills. Above all, they are apt to be self-centered and self-absorbed, with little interest in their neighbors and communities....

They are more restless, more sybaritic, and less social than most Americans are. They tend to like fine restaurants a lot more than off-road driving, seldom go to church and have limited interest in doing volunteer work to help others.

David Bostwick, the director of market research at Chrysler, told Bradsher: "We have a basic resistance in our society to admitting that we are parents, and no longer able to go out and find another mate. If you have a sport utility, you can have the smoked windows, put the children in the back and pretend you're still single."

Bostwick says that compared to those who buy similarly large minivans, SUV drivers are selfish:

Sport utility people say, "I already have two kids, I don't need 20." Then we talk to the people who have minivans and they say, "I don't have two kids, I have 20 — all the kids in the neighborhood."

One of General Motors' top engineers also spoke of the difference between minivanners and

SUVers: "SUV owners want to be more like, 'I'm in control of the people around me.'" He went on:

With the sport utility buyers, it's more of an image thing. Sport utility buyers tend to be more like, "I wonder how people view me," and are more willing to trade off flexibility or functionality to get that.

The executive VP for North American auto operations at Honda revealed: "The people who buy SUVs are in many cases buying the outside first and then the inside. They are buying the image of the SUV first, and then the functionality."

Jim Bulin, a former Ford strategist who started his own marketing firm, told Bradsher: "It's about not letting anything get in your way and, in the extreme, about intimidating others to get out of your way." Daniel A. Gorell, who also used to market for Ford and now has his own firm, says simply that SUV drivers are "less giving, less oriented toward others."

Defenders of SUVs have attacked Bradsher for reporting these things, but they always forget the crucial point: Bradsher isn't the one slamming SUV owners — it's the auto industry itself. ⌗

47
THE WORD "SQUAW" IS NOT A DERISIVE TERM FOR THE VAGINA

It's widely believed that "squaw" is a crude word for the vagina. Whether people under this misapprehension believe that the word is Native American (specifically from the Mohawk language) or was made up by Europeans, they think that calling a woman "squaw" is the same as calling her "cunt." Activists are on a crusade to stamp out the word, which is part of over 1,000 placenames in the United States, and they've met with some success. A 1995 Minnesota law, for example, ordered the changing of all geographical names containing the misunderstood word.

William Bright — UCLA professor emeritus of linguistics and anthropology, and editor of the book *Native American Placenames of the United States* — writes:

All linguists who have commented on the word "squaw," including specialists on Indian languages and on the history of American vocabulary, agree that it is not from Mohawk, or any other Iroquoian language. Rather, the word was borrowed as early as 1624 from Massachusett, the language of Algonquians in the area we now call Massachusetts; in that language it meant simply "young woman."

Several languages of the Algonquian family — including Cree, Objibwa, and Fox — still use similar words for "woman."

The confusion might have come from the fact that the Mohawk word for a woman's naughty bits is "otsískwa." But since Mohawk belongs to a different language family (Iroquois), the etymologies of the words are completely separate. Bright notes that current speakers of Mohawk don't consider "squaw" in any way related to their word for vagina.

Still, there is no doubt that "squaw" has been used as an epithet by white people, starting at least in the 1800s. It even appears this way in the work of James Fenimore Cooper. However, given its meaning of "woman," when used in a mean-spirited way, it's probably more equivalent to "broad" or "bitch" than to "cunt." Even this is a corruption of the word's true definition.

The many places across the US with names incorporating "squaw" were labeled that way to *honor* female chiefs or other outstanding Native women, or because women performed traditional activities at these locations. In an essay that earned her death threats, Abenaki storyteller and historical consultant Marge Bruchac wrote:

Any word can hurt when used as a weapon. Banning the word will not erase the past, and will only give the oppressors power to define our language. What words will be next? Pappoose? Sachem? Pow Wow? If we accept the slander, and internalize the insult, we discredit our female ancestors who felt no shame at hearing the word spoken. To ban indigenous words discriminates against Native people and their languages. Are we to be condemned to speaking only the "King's English?" What about all the words from other Native American languages?....

When I hear it ["squaw"] spoken by Native peoples, in its proper context, I hear the voices of the ancestors. I am reminded of powerful grandmothers who nurtured our people and fed the strangers, of proud women chiefs who stood up against them, and of mothers and daughters and sisters who still stand here today. ♀

48
YOU CAN MAIL LETTERS FOR LITTLE OR NO COST

I may never receive another piece of mail, but I have to let you in on a secret: It's possible to send letters for free or for well below current postage rates. Information on beating the postal system has been floating around for decades, but it wasn't gathered in one place until outlaw publisher Loompanics put forth *How To Screw the Post Office* by "Mr. Unzip" in 2000.

Not content to theorize from an ivory tower, Unzip put these methods through the ultimate real-world test: He mailed letters. He also examined the envelopes in which hundreds upon hundreds of cust-omers had paid their utility bills. Based on this, he offers proof that letters with insufficient postage often make it to their destinations.

The key is that the machines which scan for stamps work incredibly fast, processing ten letters per second. They're also fairly unsophisticated in their detection methods, relying mainly on stamps' glossy coating as a signal. Because of this, it's possible to successfully use lower-rate stamps, including outdated stamps, postcard stamps, and even 1-cent stamps. Beyond that, Unzip successfully sent letters affixed with only the perforated edges from a block of stamps. Even those pseudostamps sent by charities like Easter Seals or environmental groups can fool the scanners.

Another approach is to cut stamps in half, using each portion as full postage. Not only does this give you two stamps for the price of one, but you can often salvage the uncancelled portion of stamps on letters you receive. In fact, the author shows that sometimes the Post Office processes stamps that have already been fully cancelled. This happens more often when the ink is light, but even dark cancellation marks aren't necessarily a deal-breaker.

Then there's the biggie, the Post Office's atomic secret that lets you mail letters for free. Say you're sending a letter to dear old mom. Simply put mom's address as the return address. Then write your address in the center of the envelope, where you'd normally put hers. Forget about the stamp. The letter will be "returned" to her for insufficient postage.

Unzip covers further techniques involving stamp positioning, metered mail, 2-cent stamps, and other tricks. Except perhaps for the reversed address scam, none of these tricks will guarantee your missive gets to its destination, so you wouldn't want to try them with important letters. But if you want to save a few cents once in a while — or more likely, you want to have fun hacking the postal system — it can be done. ⌁

49
ADVERTISERS' INFLUENCE ON THE NEWS MEDIA IS WIDESPREAD

In 1995, the *San Jose Mercury News* almost went under because of a boycott by all of its car company advertisers. Why were they so irate? The *Merc* had published an article telling consumers how to negotiate a better price with car dealers.

When the executive editor of the *Chicago Sun-Times*, Larry Green, was challenged for displaying editorial favoritism toward advertisers, he openly declared: "We have to take care of our customers."

Tales like this bubble up every once in a while, so it shouldn't come as a shock that advertisers sometimes try to influence the news outlets that run their ads. The real shock is how often this happens.

In its 2002 survey, the Project for Excellence in Journalism asked 103 local TV newsrooms across the US about pressure from sponsors:

In all, 17 percent of news directors say that sponsors have discouraged them from pursuing stories (compared to 18 percent last year), and 54 percent have been pressured to cover stories about sponsors, up slightly from 47 percent last year.

Of the stations that investigated auto companies that were sponsors, half suffered economically for it, usually by the withdrawal of advertising. One car company cancelled $1 million of ads it had planned with a station.

In a classic 1992 survey (that desperately needs to be repeated), Marquette University's Department of Journalism tallied questionnaire results from 147 editors of daily newspapers. Among the findings:

■ 93.2 percent said sponsors had "threatened to withdraw advertising from [the] paper because of the content of the stories." (89 percent replied that the advertisers followed through on this threat.)

■ 89.9 percent responded that advertisers had "tried to influence the content of a news story or feature."

■ 36.7 percent said that advertisers had "succeeded in influencing news or features in [the] newspaper."

■ 71.4 percent said that "an advertiser tried to kill a story at [the] newspaper."

■ 55.1 percent revealed that they had gotten "pressure from within [the] paper to write or tailor news stories to please advertisers."

In the decade since this poll, the media have become even more corporate and more consolidated, so it's hard to imagine that the situation has improved. ⌁

50
THE WORLD'S MUSEUMS CONTAIN INNUMERABLE FAKES

The next time you're marveling at a painting by Picasso, a statue by Michelangelo, or a carving from ancient Egypt, don't be absolutely sure that you're looking at the genuine article. Art fakery has been around since ancient times and is still in full swing — museums, galleries, and private collections around the world are stocked with phonies. This fact comes to us from an insider's insider — Thomas Hoving, former director of the Metropolitan Museum of Art in New York City. In his book *False Impressions: The Hunt for Big-Time Art Fakes*, he writes:

The fact is that there are so many phonies and doctored pieces around these days that at times, I almost believe that there are as many bogus works as genuine ones. In the decade and a half that I was with the Metropolitan Museum of Art I must have examined fifty thousand works in all fields. Fully 40 percent were either phonies or so hypocritically restored or so misattributed that they were just the same as forgeries. Since then I'm sure that that percentage has risen. What few art professionals seem to want to admit is that the art world we are living in today is a new, highly active, unprincipled one of art fakery.

Ancient Egyptian objects are particularly likely to be bogus. Furthermore, Hoving estimates that the fraud rate for religious artifacts from pagan and early Christian times is literally 99 percent. As many as 5,000 fake Dürers were created after the master's death, and half of Vienna master Egon Schiele's pencil drawings are fakes.

But it isn't just current con artists making this junk; the ancients did it, too. For around a millennia, Romans couldn't get enough of Greek statues, gems, glasses, and other objects, so forgers stepped in to fill the demand. Hoving writes:

The volume was so great that Seneca the Elder (ca. 55 BC – AD 39) is recorded by a contemporaneous historian as remarking that there were no fewer than half a dozen workshops in the first century AD working full time in Rome on just colored gems and intaglios. Today it's almost impossible to tell what's genuinely ancient Greek and what's Roman fakery, because those gems and intaglios are made of material that dates to ancient times and the style is near perfect.

Art forgery isn't the realm of nobodies, either. During certain periods of their lives, Renaissance masters Donatello and Verochio put bread on the table by creating *faux* antiquities. Rubens painted copies of earlier artists. El Greco's assistants created five or six copies of their boss' work, each of which was then passed off as the original (and they're still wrongly considered the originals).

Hoving reveals that pretty much every museum has at one time or another been suckered into buying and displaying fakes, and many are still showing them. Of course, most of the examples he uses are from the Met, but he also says that phony works still sit in the Louvre, the Getty, the British Museum, the Museum of Fine Arts, Boston, and the Vatican, among others. (Hoving estimates that 90 percent of the ancient Roman statues in the Holy See's collection are actually eighteenth-century European knock-offs.)

Revealing further examples, the *Independent* of London catalogs three Goyas in the Met that are now attributed to other artists; Rodin sketches actually done by his mistress; Fragonard's popular *Le baiser à la dérobée* (*The Stolen Kiss*), which seems to have been painted by his sister-in-law; and many Rubens works actually created by the artist's students. According to the newspaper: "The Rembrandt Research Committee claims that most works attributed to Rembrandt were in fact collaborative studio pieces."

It's enough to make you question the ceiling of the Sistine Chapel. ☐

51
MEN HAVE CLITORISES

It's long been noted that all of us start in the womb as sexless little blobs. We each had the same undifferentiated external equipment (a bud of tissue), plus two sets of internal ducts.

Depending on whether an embryo has a Y sex chromosome or two X's, during week seven it starts developing into a boy or a girl. That little mound of tissue (the genital tubercle) either opens to form two sets of labia and a clitoris, or it closes to make a penis and testicles. When viewed this way, the similarities between guys' and dolls' private parts is obvious and has drawn comments since ancient Greek times.

But there's a whole lot more overlap than you might suspect. Women aren't the only ones who have a clitoris. Men do, too.

To fully understand this, it helps to know some things about our naughty bits. In women, the clit is a much larger organ than it generally gets credit for being. That little bit of ultrasensitive tissue that is the target of so much attention is merely the tip of the iceberg. The visible part that is touched and tasted is the crown, typically 0.25 to 0.75 of an inch in length. Hidden from view is the other 2.75 to 5 inches of the structure! The entire thing is shaped like a Y, with the visible crown leading to the section called the body, which then splits into two legs that hug the urethra and vagina canal.

This 3- to 5.75-inch structure is made of two sandwiched strips of *corpora cavernosa*, a tissue that engorges with blood and stiffens when its owner is aroused.

Turning to the penis, we see that its insides are made up of two kinds of tissue. The thin *corpus spongiosum* runs along the underside of the shaft, enveloping the urethra, and accounts for all of the head. This tissue plays a minor role in erections, since a hard-on is due mostly to the two sandwiched strips of *corpora cavernosa*, which comprise the bulk of the shaft. These taper off internally right as they reach the *spongiosum* dickhead.

As in women, a man's *cavernosa* soaks up blood and becomes erect when sexually excited. As in women, the *cavernosa* is shaped like a Y with three parts — crown, body, legs. In the case of men, the body accounts for more of the structure, and the legs are relatively stubby. On average, the male *cavernosa* is typically longer and thicker (which makes sense, since men as a group are bigger than women), and — unlike women — the majority of it is visible.

So here's what we have: the same tissue forming the same structure in the same place. In other words, it's the same thing.

A penis is really a clitoris that's been pulled mostly out of the body and grafted on top of a much smaller piece of *spongiosum* containing the urethra. 🗘

As much as I'd like to be known as the person who first realized that men have clits, the credit goes to psychologist-anatomist-sexologist Josephine Lowndes Sevely for first making this explicit in 1987. Science writer Catherine Blackledge expanded on it in 2004.

52
OUT OF EVERY 100 PEOPLE, TEN WEREN'T FATHERED BY THE MAN THEY BELIEVE IS DAD

Geneticists, disease researchers, and evolutionary psychologists have known it for a while, but the statistic hasn't gotten much air outside of the ivory tower. Consistently, they find that one in ten of us wasn't fathered by the man we think is our biological dad.

Naturally, adoptees and stepchildren realize their paternal situation. What we're talking about here is people who have taken it as a given, for their entire lives, that dear old Dad is the one who contributed his sperm to the process. Even Dad himself may be under this impression. And Mom, knowing it's not a sure thing, just keeps quiet.

Genetic testing companies report that almost one-third of the time, samples sent to them show that the man is not father to the child. But these companies are used when there's a court order in a paternity suit or when a man gets suspicious because his kid looks a lot like his best friend or his wife's coworker. So we shouldn't be surprised that the non-paternity rate for these tests hovers around 30 percent.

The shocker comes when we look at the numbers for accidental discoveries, those that occur when paternity isn't thought to be an issue. Sometimes this happens on an individual basis; other times, due to large-scale studies of blood types, disease susceptibility, kinship, and other fields of medical and scientific investigation.

Dr. Caoilfhionn Gallagher of the University College Dublin gives an example of the former:

The paradigmatic situation is that three people come to a hospital together, a husband, wife and their child who they fear has cystic fibrosis. If the child has the incurable disease she must have received two copies of the CF gene, one from each parent. Tests at the hospital confirm the family's worst fears — she has the disease — but also reveal something unexpected. The child's mother carries one of the culprit genes, but the father's DNA shows no such sign, which means he is not the carrier and therefore cannot possibly be her biological father.

The latter type of discovery occurred in *the* classic case from the early 1970s. Scientists were eyeballing blood types in the British town of West Isleworth, taking the red stuff from entire families. They realized, to their dismay, that fully 30 percent of the children had blood types which proved that they couldn't possibly be biologically related to their "fathers." The true rate of illegitimacy was still higher, though, because even some fathers and bastards would have matching blood types due to coincidence. The researchers estimated that the true rate was around 50 percent.

Other studies have found a 20-30 percent rate in Liverpool, 10 percent in rural Michigan, and 2.3 percent among native Hawaiians. The overall figure of 10 percent is actually an average estimate based on many studies taking place in sundry regions over the course of decades. In his book *Sperm Wars: The Science of Sex*, biologist Robin Baker, PhD, summarizes the stats:

Actual figures range from 1 percent in high-status areas of the United States and Switzerland, to 5 to 6 percent for moderate-status males in the United States and Great Britain, to 10 to 30 percent for lower-status males in the United States, Great Britain and France.

The prestigious medical journal *The Lancet* concurs: "The true frequency of non-paternity is not known, but published reports suggest an incidence from as low as 1% per generation up to about 30% in the population."

The research shows that the lower a purported father's socioeconomic status, the more likely his wife got someone else to father the child. From a Darwinian standpoint this makes perfect sense, since she wants her offspring to have the highest-caliber DNA, which may not come from the stiff she settled for at the altar.

This knowledge should make Father's Day a much more interesting, and introspective, holiday

53
HARDCORE SEXUAL IMAGERY IS AS OLD AS THE HUMAN RACE

Sometimes it's directly spoken, and sometimes it floats unsaid in the background — the idea that visual hardcore pornography is something unique to our decadent, modern society. Only in the past few decades have graphic representations of sex sprung into existence, according to this naïve belief. These things would send our innocent forebears into cardiac arrest. Whether you dig porn or whether you think it's filth that's rotting our sick society (or both), there's a tendency to view it in an ahistorical vacuum. Visuals depicting full-penetration sex acts, engorged penises, and/or spread-open labia made their appearance in the mists of prehistory and have never gone away.

Cave and rock drawings around the world limn the real or imagined doings of our ancestors. The famous rock art at Fezzan in the Sahara Desert, dated to about 5000 BC, shows manimal hybrids with enormous schlongs, some almost as big as the rest of their bodies. In some scenes, they're penetrating spread women. Caves in Italy, Spain, Russia, India, and Mesopotamia also portray Neandertals boffing. A drawing of doggie-style sex in a French cave has been dated to 40,000 BC.

China has contributed a considerable amount of sex imagery to the world, including coins showing gods and goddesses screwing, minted during the Han Dynasty (206 BC – 220 AD), and the illustrated "pillow books" from the nineteenth century.

The ancient Greeks drenched their vases, plates, goblets, and other objects with a litany of anal, oral, and vaginal sex — two men doing a woman or a third guy from both ends, young mixed-sex couples, old men and young boys, men with animals, women loving women, satyrs fucking nubile flesh.

When the ruins of Pompeii were excavated, Victorian archaeologists must've gone white when confronted with frescos showing the same things that fascinated the Greeks, only these were rendered in a realistic style using full color. When the relics were put on display in Naples National Museum, not all of them made the cut. The dildos, fornicating frescoes, some statues (like the one of a satyr humping a goat), and other explicit works were kept in a secret room that was sealed off from the public for around 200 years.

The Egyptians were no prudes, either. Pharaohs were sometimes rendered with rock-hard stiffies, and the Ani Papyrus shows us how they got that way: A woman kneels before the pharaoh, giving him a blowjob in a ritual known as the animation of the phallus (in the porn industry, she'd be called a fluffer). Other artwork shows women, bent at the waist, being penetrated by guys with impossibly long, thin dicks.

Engravings for bawdy Medieval literary masterpieces such as *The Decameron* and *Gargantua and Pantagruel* could still make people blush. The same can be said of the hardcore etchings and engravings that flourished during the Renaissance and into the 1700s. A series of etchings accompanying a Dutch edition of de Sade's *Juliette* may still be unrivaled for the sheer inventiveness and scope of the clusterfucks they depict.

If you thought that sexual photography started with *Playboy* and cheesecake in the 1950s, you're off by a full century. Daguerreotypes of naked women started showing up in the late 1840s in France, not long after the process was unveiled in 1839. At first, the images were the exclusive playthings of the rich, but the photographers quickly realized that a huge market existed for their work, triggering a tsunami of mass-produced images starting in the 1850s.

Though many of the women in these shots appear demure and adopt poses from classical art, the nudity is fully frontal. Some of these old photos dispense with coyness altogether — what we would today call a split-beaver shot appeared in 1851. That same time period saw photos of women giving each other enemas. Pictures of ladies flagellating each other arrived only a few years later, as did images of women being penetrated by stiff cocks. Although rare at first, these pictures of sex and genitals became more common as the decades progressed. One of the most popular of the erotic photos carried by soldiers during the US Civil War was a shot of a woman whole-heartedly spreading her legs right at the camera.

History professor Jonathan Coopersmith writes: "The scale of production of photographs, postcards and slides was enormous: an 1874 police raid on London pornographer Henry Haylor found 130,248 obscene photos and 5,000 obscene slides."

Photos of nekkid dudes took longer to reach the masses. Shutterbugs were snapping pics of nude men in the 1850s for painters to use as reference, but it wasn't until close to 1900 that these photos "for the use of artists" (nudge, wink) were sold on a much wider basis.

The first porn film was created in 1896, not long after the invention of motion picture technology as we know it. "Stag films" soon became an underground sensation, with informal gatherings of men watching these hardcore sex flicks that had been shot on 8 mm or 16 mm film. The Kinsey Institute's collection holds 1,697 of these nuggets going all the way back to 1913.

Still photography and film continued to be used for the creation of one-handed material during the entire twentieth century, finally going mainstream with *Playboy*, *Penthouse*, *I Am Curious (Yellow)*, *Deep Throat*, the VCR, and the Internet.

A menace to society? Hardcore sex imagery has been around continuously since some troglodyte first scribbled on a cave wall, yet somehow the human race survives. ♡

54
SHAKESPEARE'S WORKS ARE LOADED WITH SEXUAL JOKES AND TERMS

For almost all of us, our only exposure to Shakespeare's writings came in high school and college. Which means that we probably never heard that his work is rife with sexual puns and imagery, since teachers and professors aren't too quick to mention this aspect of the Bard. Besides a general taboo against sexual matters (not to mention fear of being censured by school boards or faculty committees, or even sued by bluenose students), the whitewashing is done for the same reason it's always done — to protect reputations, in this case Shakespeare's. Instructors are trying as hard as they can to convince impressionable minds of Shakespeare's genius and importance, so it wouldn't do to tell them that the greatest writer in the English language played around with "fuck," "cunt," and "prick." Haven't we been told that only people with no imagination and poor vocabularies resort to such foul language?

Shakespeare was enamored with vaginas. In his groundbreaking work, *Shakespeare's Bawdy*, mainstream scholar Eric Partridge lists 68 terms that the Bard used in both direct references and double *entendres*: "bird's nest," "box unseen," "crack," "flower," "forfended place," "hole," "nest of spicery," "Netherlands," "O," "Pillicock-hill," "salmon's tail," "secret parts," "Venus' glove," "withered pear," "wound," and dozens more.

Penises didn't rank quite as high in Shakespeare's mind, but Partridge still finds 45 dick euphemisms in the works, including "bugle," "dart of love," "instrument," "little finger," "loins," "pizzle," "potato-finger," "thorn," and "tool."

Some of Shakespeare's indecencies are lost on us moderns. But when you learn that "to die" also meant to orgasm, you get the joke in *Much Ado About Nothing* when Benedick tells his ladylove: "I will live in thy heart, die in thy lap, and be buried in thy eyes."

Sometimes it's not that subtle, like when Mercutio tells the Nurse in *Romeo and Juliet* that "the bawdy hand of the dial is now upon the prick of noon." Besides the overt imagery of a "bawdy hand" on a "prick," Shakespeare's also making a sly reference to the hands of a clock being straight up at 12 o'clock.

William even invented a highly visual slang term for sex that's still in use. In *Othello*, Iago informs Brabantio: "I am one, sir, that comes to tell you your daughter and the Moor [i.e., Othello] are now making the beast with two backs."

The Bard never directly used the word "fuck," but he did pun on it. In *The Merry Wives of Windsor*, as Sir Hugh Evans tries to teach Latin, a bizarre speech impediment involving the letter "V" makes him talk about the "focative" case. This is immediately followed by him mentioning the Latin word *caret* (a homophone of "carrot"), which a female character assures us is "a good root."

The word also makes a disguised appearance in *Henry V*. Act 3, scene 4 is delivered almost entirely in French, and its sole purpose is to lead up to a linguistic sex joke. Katherine asks Alice to tell her the English words for various body parts (elbow, nails, etc.). Toward the end, she wants to know how to say *"le pied et la robe"* ("foot and dress") in English. Alice tells her that they're "foot" and "coun" (she means "gown" but badly mispronounces it). Katherine mistakes this for the French words meaning "fuck" (*foutre*) and "cunt" (*con*), leading her to screech — in French — that those words "should not be used by a lady-in-waiting."

"Cunt" makes another appearance — punned in the word "country" — in this exchange from *Hamlet*, in which Ophelia thinks the Dane is aiming to get some nookie:

Hamlet: Lady, shall I lie in your lap?
Ophelia: No, my lord.
Hamlet: I mean, my head upon your lap?
Ophelia: Ay, my lord.
Hamlet: Do you think I meant country matters?

Perhaps funniest of all, we have the scene from *Twelfth Night* in which Malvolio reads a letter and thinks the handwriting is that of Olivia, the object of his love. He exclaims that "these be her very C's, her U's and her T's and thus makes she her great P's." Apparently, the word "and" should be pronounced lazily, so that it sounds like "N" and completes the word. We even get a bonus excretory joke when Malvolio says that Olivia urinates ("P's") profusely with her cunt.

That Shakespeare! You can't turn your back on him for a minute. ⟁

55
BARBIE IS BASED ON A GERMAN SEX DOLL

The world's most famous doll — that twentieth century icon, Barbie — didn't just appear full-blown from the mind of her creator, Ruth Handler. Barbie's inspiration, her immediate predecessor, is an overtly sexual hottie named Lilli.

Lilli started out as a cartoon character drawn by Reinhard Beuthien for the Hamburg tabloid newspaper *Bild-Zeitung*. This blonde, curvy bombshell who pursued rich men first appeared in ink in 1952. Three years later, she became a plastic doll in Germany. The definitive history *Forever Barbie* reveals: "The doll, sold principally in tobacco shops, was marketed as a sort of three-dimensional pinup. ... Lilli was never intended for children: She was a pornographic caricature, a gag gift for men..." Mattel engineer Jack Ryan once called Lilli a "hooker or an actress between performances."

Ruth Handler — she and her husband were cofounders of Mattel — wanted to create a three-dimensional, plastic, grown-up doll for girls, but the company's all-male board nixed the idea. While in Europe, she happened upon the vixenish Lilli and knew that she had discovered the literal prototype for her unrealized doll. The original Barbies were deliberately based on the German mantrap (Barb's head, in fact, was cast from Lilli's with a few minor tweaks).

When the first Barbie appeared in 1959, it was as if Lilli had been cloned. They had the same puckered, fire-engine red lips, same arched eyebrows, same almond-shaped eyes glancing sidelong, same golden hair pulled into a ponytail, same height (11.5 inches), same pencil-thin legs, same wasp waist with pneumatic breasts above and child-bearing hips below.

Barbie's similarity to her slutty forerunner didn't go unnoticed. During pre-release market testing, mothers complained about Barbie's sex vibe, saying things like, "I don't like that influence on my little girl," and, "They could be a cute decoration for a man's bar." Sears — purveyors of the almighty Christmas "Wishbook" — refused to carry her at first. Nonetheless, Barbie instantly became a huge hit with girls, and Mattel spent the early years making her less of a tart. Now, every second of the day, two Barbies are sold. Lilli must be green with envy. ☿

56
FETUSES MASTURBATE

In 1996, two ob-gyns in Italy published a letter in the *American Journal of Obstetrics and Gynecology*. The heart of the matter was this:

We recently observed a female fetus at 32 weeks' gestation touching the vulva with the fingers of the right hand. The caressing movements were centered primarily on the region of the clitoris. Movements stopped after 30 to 40 seconds and started again after a few minutes. Furthermore, these slight touches were repeated and were associated with short, rapid movements of pelvis and legs. After another break, in addition to this behavior, the fetus contracted the muscles of the trunk and limbs, and then clonicotonic movements [ie, prolonged spasms] of the whole body followed. Finally, she relaxed and rested.

We observed this behavior for about 20 minutes. The mother was an active and interested witness, conversing with observers about her child's experience.

They drew the conclusion: "The female sexual response is separate from reproductive functions and doesn't need a full sexual maturity to be explicit."

The Italians also noted: "Evidence of male fetuses' excitement reflex in utero, such as erection or 'masturbation' movements, has been previously reported." This is a reference to a letter by Dr. Israel Meizner, published in the *Journal of Ultrasound Medicine*, in which the fetal ultrasound expert spies on an unborn boy bopping his baloney.

In 1995, the British science series *Equinox* achieved a first when it broadcast ultrasound footage of another male fetus playing with himself.

Sadly, a literature search shows that no one has yet published a full-fledged study of zesty zygotes, but the field is ripe for study. Dean Edell, MD (a/k/a, "America's doctor") has written: "It is common during second trimester ultrasonography examinations to see the fetus touch itself repeatedly and rhythmically on the genitalia, offering fairly compelling proof that masturbation is rooted not in sin but in biology." ⌧

57
SOME LEGAL, READILY AVAILABLE SUBSTANCES CAN GET USERS HIGH

As hard as it is to believe, the Drug Warriors have actually neglected to outlaw some common substances that can alter consciousness in a pleasurable way. As you might guess, the high from some of these goodies often leaves much to be desired when compared with their *verboten* cousins, but people who are desperate, gun-shy, or out to experience everything they can often indulge in them. We draw attention to these under-the-radar substances not to suggest that you try them but to thumb our noses at the arrogant thugs who tell us what we can and can't put into our bodies.

Nutmeg. Ingesting the proper dose of this spice can lead to a day and a half of pleasant experiences. Or not. Users seem to agree that it takes one or two hours for the first stage to hit, which may be a buzz, mellowness, or grogginess. After another few hours reality

| ...YOU'RE NOT SUPPOSED TO KNOW

seems altered — nutmeggers experience visuals, mild hallucinations, a dreamlike state, zoning out, "lucid day-dreaming," maybe even bliss. For the entire next day, trippers are languid and drowsy. But some people don't get much out of it except for feeling dizzy and tired, while others have bad reactions including racing heart and bazooka-barfing. One dissatisfied customer on the Web ended his experience with: "I'd seriously rather eat shit."

Catnip. Not just for felines anymore, catnip reportedly will give you a low-grade pot-like buzz if smoked. Experienced puffers say it works better when mixed with tobacco.

Lettuce opium. All permutations of lettuce contain an opium-like alkaloid called lactucarium. For decades, people in search of a cheap legal high have liquefied whole heads of lettuce, letting the juice evaporate and gel into a gummy substance, which is then toked. As catnip is to weed, so lettuce opium is to poppy opium — a pale imitation but better than nothing.

Cough syrup. "Doing 'tussin" — chugging cough syrup, such as Robotussin, containing the suppressant DXM — is quite popular with the legal high crowd, since you can get the goods at any drug store, and who's going to question a bottle of it in your medicine cabinet? Like nutmeg, user reports range from practically achieving nirvana to being dragged through the slimiest pits of hell. The high number of negative reports from users is a red flag.

Poppies. Going into a flower shop or an arts-and-crafts store to score might seem strange, but many of these places sell poppies. As in opium poppies. Growing the flowers is legal for the most part, but taking any steps to harvest the opium isn't. Still, the pods can be ground up and brewed to make poppy tea, while a small number of people steep the seeds in lemon juice and drink the resulting grog. Not that this is a good idea, since addiction to opiates is a hellish nightmare, but it can be done.

Nitrous oxide. Next to the flower shop with poppies is a kitchen supply or gourmet food store (who knew the mall was such a den of inequity?). They carry nitrous oxide chargers, the stuff that puts the fluff into homemade whipped cream. On the street, these palm-sized tubes are called "whippits," and the nitrous — "laughing gas" from the dentist's office — can be discharged into a heavy-duty balloon or a gadget known as a cracker, from whence it is inhaled. (Trying to suck the gas straight from the charger results in damaging skin freeze.)

Solvents and jimsonweed. As a friend of mine has said, if you're thinking of huffing solvents or ingesting jimsonweed, you might as well just bash yourself in the head with a hammer. It produces the same basic "altered state" with about as much damage.

Finally, I'd be remiss if I didn't give at least a passing mention to those three super-legal drugs: caffeine, tobacco, and alcohol…. ⌗

58
A DEA JUDGE RULED THAT POT IS MEDICALLY BENEFICIAL

For two years starting in 1986, the Drug Enforcement Administration held historic hearings aimed at the possible rescheduling of marijuana, which was and still is laughably designated as a Schedule I drug, along with heroin, ecstasy, LSD, and mescaline.

According to federal law, a substance is put on Schedule I — the most stringent level of control — if it "has a high potential for abuse," "has no currently accepted medical use in treatment in the United States," and there exists "a lack of accepted safety for use of the drug or other substance under medical supervision." Since marijuana is a nontoxic, nonaddictive plant with a millennia-long history of health uses, it utterly fails to deserve a spot in Schedule I.

Under the Controlled Substances Act, parties can petition for rescheduling of any substance, and the DEA must formally consider the request. The National Organization for the Reform of Marijuana Law and thirteen individuals with various medical conditions went through the steps to move weed to the slightly less draconian Schedule II, where it would still be considered a generally evil, destructive substance but could be more widely used for medical purposes. It took three lawsuits and two direct court orders to force the DEA to hold hearings.

During the proceedings, patients and family members testified about pot's near-miraculous ability to take away the overwhelming nausea caused by chemotherapy, its deflating of the internal eye pressure that causes glaucoma, its merciful relief of chronic pain and itching, and the way it tames spasticity. The mother of a teenager who died of testicular cancer told how chemo would make him violently vomit and dry heave for days, but if he smoked chronic before and after therapy, he'd eat dinner with the family that very night. She said: "It was clear to us that marijuana was the safest, most benign drug he received during the course of his battle against cancer."

Bunches of doctors — including oncologists, ophthalmologists, psychiatrists, and alternative health guru Andrew Weil, MD — testified on the benefits of *Cannabis sativa*. Cancer doctor Ivan Silverberg, MD, declared under oath: "It [using marijuana] has simply become a standard routine, accepted as part of the practice of Oncology."

Seventy-two articles from medical journals were placed into the record. NORML entered into evidence a list of 33 states that passed statutes recognizing pot's medicinal value.

On the side of the DEA and other Drug Warriors, a number of heartless doctors repeated the prohibitionist mantras that pot is no more effective than synthetic THC (to which patients who've tried both unanimously say bullshit) and that there's not enough scientific evidence to support pot's efficacy (never mind the fact that its illegality makes it almost impossible to scientifically study).

In the end, the DEA's administrative judge ruled in favor of sanity and compassion: He decreed that marijuana should be moved to Schedule II, where it can be widely used under a doc's care. In his ruling, Judge Francis L. Young wrote:

Marijuana, in its natural form, is one of the safest therapeutically active substances known to man. By any measure of rational analysis marijuana can be

safely used within a supervised routine of medical care. ...

The evidence in this record clearly shows that marijuana has been accepted as capable of relieving the distress of great numbers of very ill people, and doing so with safety under medical supervision. It would be unreasoning, arbitrary and capricious for [the] DEA to continue to stand between those sufferers and the benefit of this substance in light of the evidence on record.

Such enlightened thinking could not be allowed to stand, of course. The head of the DEA simply rejected his own judge's ruling, and there the matter ended. ▫

59
EACH MONTH, NEW WARNINGS ARE ADDED TO THE LABELS OF 40 DRUGS

Every month, the FDA posts a list of all drugs that have had "safety labeling changes to the contraindications, boxed warning, warnings, precautions, or adverse reactions sections." In other words, these drugs are more dangerous, and dangerous in different ways, than their makers knew (or admitted) when they were declared fit for the American public. Now the pharmaceutical corporations have been forced to tell us about more dangers, problems, contraindications, and side effects regarding the products that millions of people are already using.

During 2003 and the first five months of 2004, an average of 40 drugs received revised labels each month, for an average of almost two every business day. May 2004 produced the highest number, a bumper crop of 65 new warnings, while March of that year came in second, with 59.

Even the massively marketed drugs that have become household names get hit. Clarinex, Effexor, Flonase, Flovent, Nasacort, Ritalin, Xanax, Zithromax, and Zyprexa are among those with new warnings during the time period.

Suprax (cefixime) — used to treat bacterial infections — now is admitted to cause angioedema (swelling of the heart), facial edema, hepatitis, jaundice, acute renal failure, seizures, and toxic epidermal necrolysis (death of the flesh). The new label tells us: "Anaphylactic/anaphylactoid reactions (including shock and fatalities) have been reported with the use of cefixime."

Vioxx, which is supposed to treat pain, now warns that it can cause: "Migraine with or without aura." The heavily advertised allergy medication Zyrtec has been admitted to rarely cause blocking of the liver's bile ducts, swelling of the kidneys, destruction of red blood cells, hepatitis, involuntary facial movements, severely low blood pressure, stillbirth, and "aggressive reaction and convulsions."

The "healing purple pill" Nexium had bad news after it was released, with some patients developing fatal cases of skin necrosis, not to mention nonfatal cases of pancreatitis and Stevens-Johnson syndrome. Invanz added hallucinations to its label when "post-marketing experience" showed that some patients started tripping after being injected with the antibacterial drug. Similarly, after the high blood pressure medication Atacand was already in use, it was reported to be deforming and killing fetuses. Merck had to add a new box warning to

AquaMEPHYTON — its Vitamin K1 solution — when it began killing people, especially when given intravenously.

In one of the longest lags between a drug's introduction and a new warning, Demerol, a widely used pain reliever, got a new warning in February 2003: It passes straight into mother's milk, so suckling babies are ingesting this powerful, addictive narcotic if their mommies take it. Demerol was introduced in the 1930s. It took 70 years to discover that Demmies pass unaltered into breast milk?

Perhaps most significant, in spring 2004, after years of mounting evidence, six major antidepressants (Paxil, Wellbutrin, Effexor, Serzone, Celexa, Lexapro) finally received label changes warning doctors and shrinks to monitor patients for increased suicidality when starting, increasing, or decreasing any of the drugs.

One of the scariest label changes happened to Pletal (cilostazol) Tablets, which "are used to treat intermittent claud-ication, a condition in which a person experiences pain or discomfort when walking that stops with rest." The "adverse reactions" portion of the label was updated

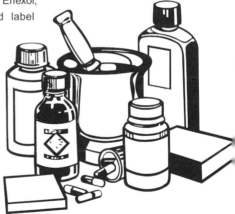

in February 2004 to include the following litany of horrors that have shown up now that the public is taking the drug:

Postmarketing Experience

The following adverse events have been reported worldwide since the launch of Pletal in the US: pain, chest pain, hot flushes, cerebral hemorrhage, angina pectoris, hypotension, hepatic dysfunction/abnormal liver function tests, jaundice, vomiting, thrombocytopenia, leukopenia, bleeding tendency, paresthesia, hyperglycemia, pulmonary hemorrhage, interstitial pneumonia, pruritus, skin eruptions including Stevens-Johnson syndrome, rash, increase BUN, and hematuria.

The following adverse events occurred outside the US prior to marketing of Pletal in the US: pulmonary hemorrhage and Stevens-Johnson syndrome.

Did you catch that last sentence? Massive bleeding of the heart and an excruciating, disfiguring skin reaction that sometimes kills you showed up *before* the drug was offered in the US. But it was sold to Americans anyway. Thanks for the warning. 🙁

60
SUVS ARE OVER 3 TIMES MORE LIKELY THAN CARS TO KILL PEDESTRIANS WHO ARE STRUCK

If you're one of the 86,500 pedestrians who get smashed by motor vehicles each year in the US, better hope it's not a "light truck" — an SUV, pickup truck, or van — that knocks you flying. These vehicles are 3.4 times as likely to kill you as a car.

In a study published in the journal *Injury Prevention*, researchers from the Universities of Washington and Virginia crunched fatality stats from six US cities, including Chicago and Seattle, which had been collected by the National Highway Safety Administration.

When they broke down the numbers by type of vehicle, sure enough, the goliaths of the road are more likely to leave corpses in their wake. They're not just twice as lethal, or even three times as lethal. They're almost three-and-a-half times as deadly. And when it comes to serious injuries that don't result in a funeral, the "light truck" rate is three times that of cars.

The numbers for the study were collected from 1994 to 1998. In the years since, SUVs and pickups have become much bigger and more powerful as consumers compete for higher status and intimidation factor. It stands to reason, then, that the lethality of these quasi-tanks has only increased. ⌂

61
ARISTOTLE SET BACK SCIENCE FOR AROUND 2,000 YEARS

Aristotle may have been a genius when it came to philosophy — especially logic — but he didn't know squat about science. Sure, we can't excel in every field we try our hand in, but Aristotle's massive errors aren't just a personal embarrassment to him — they directly hampered scientific progress for 1,800 to 2,000 years.

The problem is that from the time he was alive (the fourth century BC) until the Enlightenment, when Aristotle said something, that was the end of the argument. Isaac Asimov notes, perhaps with a tinge of jealousy: "No matter who disagreed with them, even other philosophers, Aristotle's ideas — whether right or wrong — usually won out." Chemist John Appeldoorn writes that "Aristotle's teachings were unquestioned. After eighteen centuries, universities accepted them as if they had been written in stone."

For example, Aristotle didn't believe that plants were divided into male and female sexes, so there the matter stood for two millennia, until botanists stated the obvious in the 1700s.

He was also wrong about inertia, and again the world had to wait — this time for Galileo, followed by Newton — to speak the truth that objects in motion stay in motion, while objects at rest stay at rest, unless acted upon by outside forces.

Like most Greeks, Aristotle championed the view that the Sun and planets revolved around the Earth. Copernicus (in the early 1500s) and Galileo (100 years later) had to risk their reputations and their lives to put the kibosh on that nonsense.

He further surmised that outer space was made up of 54 spheres and that there were only seven heavenly bodies, which were fixed and unchanging. This meant, for one thing, that comets had to be in Earth's atmosphere. Only in 1577 was this notion put out to pasture. Over the next 50 years, belief in the heavenly spheres faded.

Aristotle declared that heavier objects fall faster than lighter ones, an error that could've been exposed with simple experiments. It wasn't until 1,900 years later that Galileo dropped objects off the Tower of Pisa, proving that all things obey gravity at the same rate. By that time, Galileo already had been kicked out of the University of Pisa for daring to question Aristotle's theory.

Some Greeks, including Democritus and Hippocrates, surmised that the brain was the seat of thought, intelligence, and emotion. Tish-tosh, said Aristotle, it's the heart — and that became the accepted wisdom. Aristotle wrote: "The brain is an organ of minor importance, perhaps necessary to cool the blood." Because Greek physicians primarily held brain-centered views, that remained a strong undercurrent, yet Aristotle's heart view dominated until the 1500s.

A fellow Greek philosopher, Democritus, postulated that the physical world was made up of tiny pieces of matter, which he called atoms. But Aristotle pooh-poohed this ridiculous notion, causing it to languish in obscurity until the second half of the 1600s, when scientists began to resurrect it. It wasn't until the first years of the 1800s that the existence of atoms was universally accepted.

Who knows how much further science would've progressed if Aristotle had stuck to syllogisms?

62
NATIVE AMERICANS WERE KEPT AS SLAVES

When we think of US slavery, we think of Africans being forced to work in the fields and the master's house. Some mainstream sources will give a nod to enslaved white people, although they're almost always labeled with the euphemism "indentured servants." But you'll never hear about Native American slaves. Not because they didn't exist, but because they've been thrown into history's dustbin.

Columbus wasted little time before enslaving the native people on Hispaniola. The Spanish proceeded to make slaves out of the indigenous people all over the Caribbean, Latin America, Florida, and what is now the Southwestern US. The French did the same thing in Canada and Louisiana, as did the Portuguese in Brazil. From the early 1600s, the British were the primary enslavers of Indians in what we now call the Eastern US.

Native Americans were put to the lash in most colonies and territories east of the Mississippi River — including New York, Massachusetts, Rhode Island, Pennsylvania, Virginia, the Carolinas, Georgia — as well as the areas that were or became Arkansas, Kansas, Nebraska, Utah, New Mexico, and Arizona. A small number of Native Americans were taken from the West Indies to the American colonies, but by far most of the traffic was the reverse, with the mainland supplying the islands with Indian slaves to handle crops such as sugar.

How did the European colonists get their hands on Indian slaves? Many were captured directly during wars between Europeans and Native Americans. In some cases, Indians sold their children into slavery. In a third route, perhaps accounting for most slaves, Indian tribes sold their captives to the palefaces. As in Africa, slaves largely were not captured by Europeans but were snared by neighboring tribes, who then sold them to the white men. At first, Native Americans simply sold their prisoners of war, but tribes quickly started raiding other tribes for the sole purpose of snatching human chattel for the settlers.

The various European groups started using Indian slaves almost as soon as they set up settlements. The Yamasee war almost, but not quite, eliminated the practice in 1715 in the Southeast. The Spanish made slaves out of Indians in southern Mexico, continuing the practice as they pushed north of the Rio Grande, forcing their captives to work primarily in mines and as household servants. The practice slowed down a few years after the US wrested the Southwest from Mexico in 1848, but it definitely didn't stop. Even the Civil War didn't halt the practice. Immediately after the War Between the States, though, Congress took up the issue of Indian slavery in the Southwest, eventually directing William T. Sherman to liberate the captive Native Americans. (Although this effectively ended the slave trade, the practice of slaveholding didn't completely stop; a rancher in Arizona is known to have kept a female Apache, captured when she was fourteen, into the 1930s.)

In his scholarly book *The Indian Slave Trade*, history professor Alan Gallay notes: "Most Indian slaves were women and children, whereas the majority of African slaves were adult males." Native Americans generally didn't make ideal slaves for various reasons. One of the main "problems" was that they could more easily fly the coop and rejoin their tribe or at least a friendly tribe. They also had a hard time resisting all those funky European diseases. Because of this, their numbers never came close to those of African slaves.

How many Native Americans were enslaved will never be known, so we have only very rough estimates. This trade wasn't documented nearly to the extent of its African counterpart, and most of the records that were created haven't survived. Professor Gallay has assembled what pieces remain to come up with a probable range of Indians who were enslaved by the British in the Southeast up to 1715: no less than 25,000 to 32,200, and no more than 51,000. In the seriously obscure book *Indian Slave Trade in the Southwest*, L.R. Bailey cites 6,000 slaves in the territory of New Mexico when the Civil War broke out.

So we're up to 31,000 to 57,000 without including any of New England, New York, the Southeast *after* 1715, antebellum New Mexico, the rest of the Southwest, the Plains states, or the Indians enslaved by Spaniards in Florida and the French in Louisiana. And that's only part of the hemispheric picture; native peoples enslaved in Canada, Central and South America, and the Caribbean islands obviously would add lots of misery to the total. ⌕

63
GEORGE WASHINGTON EMBEZZLED GOVERNMENT FUNDS

We typically imagine George Washington to be as pure as driven snow, a demigod who won the Revolutionary War, then assumed the mantle of President to flawlessly lead a fledgling country.

The reality is vastly different. Besides being borderline incompetent on the battlefield (during the first four years of the Revolution, he lost *every* major engagement), the man who could not tell a lie started the tradition of presidential corruption.

The whistle was blown by the Clerk of Congress — writing under the *nom de plume* "A Calm Observer" — in the *Philadelphia Aurora*, a muckraking anti-federalist newspaper founded, edited, and published by Benjamin Franklin's grandson. In 1795, the *Aurora* published the Clerk's detailed breakdown of how much loot Washington had taken from the Treasury beyond his Constitutionally-sanctioned $25,000 annual salary.

According to the paperwork seen by the Clerk, the Father of Our Country started out honest, drawing exactly his salary of $25K during year one. But over the course of the second year, he took $30,150, thus embezzling $5,150. In his third year, perhaps suffering a pang on conscience, GW took a little less than his entitlement: $24,000. He made up for it during his fourth year, though, by filching an extra grand.

In February 1793, as Washington's second term was about to begin, Congress passed an act calling for the President to be paid on a quarterly basis (i.e., $6,250 every three months). But during the first quarter of his second term, Washington took $11,000 from the Treasury.

At this point, the Clerk of Congress must've lost access to the smoking guns, since he wonders whether the graft continued after Q1 of the second term. He presciently asks: "If the precedent which this donation from the treasury furnishes, were to be allowed in favour of other public officers, how many hundred thousand dollars per annum would thus be lawlessly taken from the public treasury and saddled upon the people?"

64
THE DECLARATION OF INDEPENDENCE CONTAINS A RACIALLY DEROGATORY REMARK

Wouldn't it be shocking to find that one of the United States' two most important founding documents contains a racial slur? That it denigrates lazy "darkies"? Or conniving "slant-eyes"? Or bloodthirsty "savages"?

Those first two examples aren't in the US Declaration of Independence, but the last one is. When airing their grievances against King George III, the Founders wrote:

He has excited domestic insurrections amongst us, and has endeavoured to bring on the inhabitants of our frontiers, the merciless Indian Savages, whose known rule of warfare, is an undistinguished destruction of all ages, sexes and conditions.

Of course, the truth of the matter is that some Native Americans did indeed massacre settlers. But some settlers, not to mention military troops, were also slaughtering Indians. And just who was encroaching on whom?

Now, I'm not saying we should change the Declaration; I'm opposed to revising the past, and that goes double for such a momentous document. But if I were a Native American, knowing that my country's first landmark document slurs my people wouldn't sit well.

On a related note, California's Constitution (the second version, from 1879, which is still in force) contained horrible slurs and measures against Chinese people. It specified that no private or public employer may hire Chinese, that Chinese should be thrown out of cities and towns, and that the state should bar them from entering. A particularly vicious clause called on the legislature to take action against the "burdens and evils arising from the presence of aliens who are or may become vagrants, paupers, mendicants, criminals, or invalids afflicted with contagious or infectious diseases, and from aliens otherwise dangerous or detrimental to the well-being or peace of the State." Those racist sections were soon declared unconstitutional by the courts and were struck from the constitution. ▯

65
JAMES AUDUBON KILLED ALL THE BIRDS HE PAINTED

One of America's great naturalists, John James Audubon painted highly realistic portraits of practically every type of bird in North America. The self-taught artist's resulting four-volume collection of life-size paintings, *The Birds of America* (1827–38), is regarded as both an artistic and an ornithological masterpiece, and reproductions of his work are still brightening walls around the world.

But exactly how Audubon was able to capture our feathered friends' likenesses so completely is usually glossed over. The *Encyclopedia Britannica* fails to even broach the subject. The Audubon Society's page on their namesake mentions that he loved to hunt, but the connection is never explicitly made.

Audubon shot all the birds he painted. He then used wires to pose the corpses of these hawks, falcons, partridges, sparrows, woodpeckers, and other winged creatures before putting brush to canvas. In one diary entry, he writes about sneaking up on a large group of sleeping pelicans and blasting two of them before his gun jammed and the awakened survivors took off (he was disappointed that he didn't get to kill them all). And when hunting snoozing avians in the wild was too much trouble, he resorted to other methods. He once bought a caged eagle, killed it, then captured its likeness.

One of Audubon's biographers, Duff Hart-Davis, reveals: "The rarer the bird, the more eagerly he pursued it, never apparently worrying that by killing it he might hasten the extinction of its kind."

Over 1,000 individual birds appear in Audubon's paintings, but we know that the body count is much higher. He didn't feel some kills were worthy of being painted. Others were put on canvas, but the artist was dissatisfied with his work and never displayed it. In other cases, he had already painted a specific type of bird but then found an intriguing individual variation, so he just had to blow it away.

He once wrote: "I call birds few when I shoot less than one hundred per day." 🗔

66
ONE-QUARTER OF LYNCHING VICTIMS WERE NOT BLACK

The word "lynch" has become synonymous with a white mob brutally killing a black person. The bulk of the time, lynchings did happen along those color lines. But not always. In a fourth of the known cases, a white, Asian, or Native person was the unfortunate victim.

The *Reader's Companion to American History* cites the universally referenced figures on mob hangings collected by the venerable Tuskegee Institute: "Between 1882 (when reliable statistics were first collected) and 1968 (when the classic forms of lynching had disappeared), 4,743 persons died of lynching, 3,446 of them black men and women." In other words, 27.3 percent were of other races.

The official website for the State of Texas says that in one the worst years (1885), lynch mobs in the state murdered 24 white people and 19 black people. In the year with the highest number of mob hangings (1892), 30 percent of the victims were white. In Kentucky, the overall tally was 31 percent white.

Naturally, it was almost always white mobs that killed white people, though there are a miniscule number of cases in which a black mob strung up a white person.

Also, we know of rare instances in which black mobs lynched black individuals. Eleven such incidents are known to have occurred in Georgia alone.

Most of the victims classified as "white" were US-born people of European extraction. However, this category also encompasses Mexicans (a minimum of 216 victims) and European immigrants. Some additional victims were targeted for being Jewish.

Adding further complexity are the victims of other races, including Native Americans and Chinese immigrants.

Although lynching was primarily white on black, the full picture — which has yet to be drawn but is hinted at here — shows that the contours of lynching aren't as simply rendered as we'd like to think. ♋

67
FREUD FAILED TO HELP HIS PATIENTS

In his entire fabled career — which really is mostly a fable — Freud wrote up detailed case histories of only six patients, all of them heavily spun, revised, and embellished to make Herr Doktor look like a genius. In the intervening century or more, scholars have dug up documentation — such as letters and contemporaneous case notes — which demonstrate Freud's inability to meaningfully help his patients, falling light years short of the incredible cures he claimed.

Let's start by looking at the proto-case, "Anna O." Though she wasn't Freud's patient, students of the old man study the case because Anna was treated by his mentor, Josef Breur, and the case was later written up by Freud (though both of them attached their names to it). This is the founding case of psychotherapy — it supposedly validated hypnosis, "talking cures," repression, oedipal desire, and other pillars of this approach. The official story is that Anna was intensely neurotic and Breur completely rid her of her "hysteria" through hypnosis.

In actuality, one month after therapy ended, Breur had her committed to an insane asylum, a place she would stay three more times over the next five years. Breur considered her hopeless; in a letter to his fiancée, Freud related his mentor's thoughts on Anna: "Breur is constantly talking about her, says he wishes she were dead so that the poor woman could be free of her suffering. He says that she will never be well again, that she is completely shattered." (It turns out that Breur was wrong, because Anna did recover in the very late 1880s, around six or seven years after her therapy ended.) Not only did Breur and Freud keep these facts from the public, at Freud's insistence years later they fabricated the case history to make it fit with psychoanalysis, presenting this failure as a rousing success and attributing this nonexistent triumph to approaches and theories that weren't around at the time.

Now let's consider Freud's six detailed case histories, whose pseudonyms are household names to students of psychology.

The first case that Freud publicly presented as a cure — though it was far from his first case — was that of "Rat Man" (don't you love these psychiatric soubriquets?). Rat Man was obsessively afraid that something terrible would happen to his father and girlfriend; these morbid thoughts had started after he heard about a hideous form of torture involving rats. Freud's conclusion? Rat Man was repressing his desire to buttfuck his dad and future wife because — and this was an unconfirmed guess on the shrink's part — Ratty's dad had severely punished him for masturbating as a toddler.

In the case history, Sigmund claimed to have treated Rat Man for close to a year, but from his notes we know that the length was actually six months. Though Rat Man broke off the therapy, Freud boasted that he'd perfectly cured the fellow ("the complete restoration of the patient's personality"). But immediately after writing the case history, Freud told Jung in a letter that Rat Man was still messed up.

Five-year-old "Little Hans" suddenly became deathly afraid of horses. Though considered one of Freud's meager half-dozen case histories, Hans actually was treated by his father, a Freud disciple. Sigmund supervised the case from afar, seeing Hans only once. Young Hans was pretty sure that his horse phobia was due to trauma from seeing a horse fall down in the street, but his father and Freud would have none of this poppycock. It was obvious to them that big-dicked horses represented the lad's threatening father, whom Hans believed wanted to castrate him. Meanwhile, Hans also wanted to nail his mother and kill his kid sister. When pressed about his supposed desire toward mommy, Hans repeatedly said no way. But his dad kept hectoring him and, naturally, Little Hans eventually broke down and told him what he wanted to hear. "Success!" screamed the inquisitors. Actually, Hans *did* slowly lose his fear of horses during the treatment, but no one has to been able to produce a shred of evidence that the nutty therapy had anything to do with it, that it wasn't just Hans slowly recovering from his scary equestrian encounter.

Two of Freud's principal case histories are barely worth mentioning. Regarding Sigmund's treatment of an unnamed eighteen-year-old lesbian, MIT cognitive scientist Frank Sulloway —

author of *Freud: Biologist of the Mind* — writes that it "terminated after a short time and involved no therapeutic improvement or even real treatment." In the other case, Freud diagnosed a psychotic — whom he never met — strictly through the man's published memoir. Whether his conclusions were correct or not is impossible to say, but we do know that to arrive at them Freud ignored parts of the memoir that contradicted his diagnosis and purposely misrepresented the man's dad (in the case history, Freud lauded him as an "excellent father," while simultaneously admitting that he was a "despot" in a letter to a pupil).

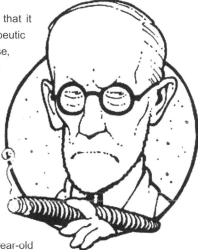

"Dora" was a depressed and "hysterical" seventeen-year-old (not eighteen, as Freud claimed) who reluctantly came to Sigmund because of problems involving friends of the family, Mr. and Mrs. K. Dora was upset because 1) Mr. K. obviously wanted a piece of her and had even made passes at her when she was thirteen and sixteen, and 2) she rightly believed that her father and Mrs. K. were getting it on. The good doctor immediately sussed what was really happening: Not only was Dora in love with Mr. K., she also wanted to give her father a blowjob and hop into the sack with *Mrs.* K. Not surprisingly, Dora thought this was a load of crap and abruptly quit seeing Freud after eleven weeks. She was still a mess when she died.

The obsessive "Wolf Man" is Freud's best-known case, most often pointed to as a shining example of psychoanalysis. The entire thing hinges on a dream that the patient had as a child: He saw white wolves sitting on top of a tree in front of his bedroom window, then woke up terrified. From this, Freud deduced that Wolfie had seen his parents humping doggie-style when he was 18 months old.

It took Freud four years to treat this poor sap, who was eventually discharged as being fully cured. Decades later, an Austrian reporter tracked him down to find out how he'd been doing since his legendary headshrinking sessions. Wolf Man called Freud's dream interpretation "terribly farfetched"; the sex-peeping scenario, which he never remembered, was "improbable"; and the universal belief that he'd been cured was "false." Turns out that he continually saw a phalanx of therapists for the rest of his life. The psychoanalysis industry actively tried to hide the miserable failure of Freud's greatest so-called success by pressuring and financially inducing Wolf Man to stay in Vienna, instead of going to the US, as he wanted, because his status as a living piece of history would bring publicity and the truth would come out. He remained a bundle of neuroses and obsessions until his death.

As leading academic Freud debunker Frederick Crews writes: "Freud was unable to document a single unambiguously efficacious treatment." ▯

68
THE BOARD GAME MONOPOLY WAS SWIPED FROM QUAKERS

Monopoly, according to its manufacturer, has been played by over 500 million people. Translated into 26 languages, as well as Braille, it's sold 200 million copies as of 1999 (the latest figures the maker has announced). Over 5 billion of those green houses have been stamped, and each year countless dead trees are turned into 500 billion dollars of rainbow-hued money.

In other words, it's a popular game. The most successful board game ever.

The official story is that a toy tinkerer named Charles Darrow from Germantown, Pennsylvania, created this billion-dollar game out of whole cloth in 1934. However, the official story is what's made from whole cloth.

When economics professor Ralph Anspach cooked up a parody game called Anti-Monopoly — the goal is to bust trusts, not build them — Parker Brothers, not surprisingly, took him to court. While researching the game's history for the lawsuit, Anspach stumbled upon the hidden truth. Using dogged detective work, he assembled the suppressed history of Monopoly.

Greatly simplified, it goes like this. The roots stretch back to the Landlord's Game, a Monopolyesque game patented in 1904 by a cross-dressing Bohemian and game-inventor named Lizzie Magie. This game mutated into a folk-game called "monopoly." As charmingly quaint as it may seem, people used to spend hour after hour playing board games with each other; they would even handmake their own copies of a game's board, cards, and pieces. From 1910 to the early 1930s, this is what happened with monopoly, mainly in the Northeastern US.

While visiting her hometown of Indianapolis, Indiana, in 1929, a Quaker teacher named Ruth Hoskins was introduced to the game by a childhood friend. She made a copy, which she took back to Atlantic City, New Jersey. Her friends and colleagues, themselves Quakers, soon decided to redo the game using places from their neck of the woods — Pacific Avenue, Park Place, the Boardwalk, etc. They also added the little hotels in addition to houses. In a crucial rule change, they removed the property auctions and gave each piece of pretend real estate a fixed value, making the game so simple that even little kids could play.

Eventually, a Quaker couple invited another couple to play the game. That's how Charles Darrow was introduced to monopoly. He showed great interest, pressing his hosts to explain all the fine points of the game. When he asked them to type up the rules and make a board for him, they thought he was a demanding bastard, but they complied. Next thing you know, Darrow is selling it as a game he "created." He had lifted the Quakers' Atlantic City version wholesale, making only some superficial changes to the game board (such as putting a colored stripe across the top of the squares instead of the original colored triangles in the bottom left corner).

He then sold it to Parker Brothers, still pretending to have invented it. The company soon discovered the ruse but went along with it, omitting and suppressing evidence of the game's true origins when they patented it under Darrow's name.

In its ruling against Parker Brothers' effort to torpedo Anti-Monopoly, the Ninth Circuit Court of

Appeals officially agreed with the facts that Anspach unearthed, declaring that the "reference to Darrow as the inventor or creator of the game is clearly erroneous." The Supreme Court upheld the decision.

Even today, Hasbro — which assimilated Parker Brothers — won't acknowledge the origins of their cash cow. They have, however, craftily modified their so-called history of Monopoly. The game's website now coyly refers to the "legend" of the game's birth, which commences when Darrow "showed" the game to the suits at Parker Brothers. They don't say that he created it, although that's the impression you'd get if you didn't know the real story. ⌑

69
GANDHI REFUSED TO LET HIS DYING WIFE TAKE PENICILLIN YET TOOK QUININE TO SAVE HIMSELF

Gandhi is often ranked, directly or subtly, alongside Jesus Christ and Martin Luther King, Jr as one of the greatest peacemakers — indeed, one of the greatest human beings — of all time. The mythology that surrounds him — which he built, leaving his followers, admirers, and hagiographers to reinforce and embellish — has almost completely smothered the many unflattering facts about him.

In such a compact book, space doesn't permit a full exploration of Gandhi's numerous, consequential skeletons — his racism toward blacks and whites, his betrayal of the Untouchables, his acquiescence toward the Nazis. Instead, let's focus on something more personal and, in some ways, more upsetting.

In August 1942, Gandhi and his wife, Kasturba, among others, were imprisoned by the British in Aga Khan Palace near Poona. Kasturba had poor circulation, and she'd weathered several heart attacks. While detained in the palace, she developed bronchial pneumonia. One of her four sons, Devadas, wanted her to take penicillin. Gandhi refused. He was okay with her receiving traditional remedies, such as water from the Ganges, but he refused her any medicines, including this newfangled antibiotic, saying that the Almighty would have to heal her.

The Life and Death of Mahatma Gandhi quotes him on February 19, 1944: "If God wills it, He will pull her through." *Gandhi: A Life* adds this wisdom from the Mahatma: "You cannot cure your mother now, no matter what wonder drugs you may muster. She is in God's hands now." Three days later, Devadas was still pushing for the penicillin, but Gandhi shot back: "Why don't you trust God?" Kasturba died that day.

The next night, Gandhi cried out: "But how God tested *my* faith!" He told one of Kasturba's doctors that the antibiotic wouldn't have saved her and that allowing her to have it "would have meant the bankruptcy of *my* faith." (Emphasis mine.)

But Gandhi's faith wasn't much of an obstacle a short time later when it was his ass on the line. A mere six weeks after Kasturba died, Gandhi was flattened by malaria. He stuck to an all-liquid diet as his doctors tried to convince him to take quinine. But Gandhi completely refused and died of the disease, right? No, actually, after three weeks of deterioration, he took the diabolical drug and quickly recovered. That stuff about trusting God's will and testing faith only applied when his wife's life hung in the balance. When he needed a drug to stave off the Grim Reaper, down the hatch it went. ⚉

70
SEVERAL THOUSAND AMERICANS WERE HELD IN NAZI CONCENTRATION CAMPS

During the Nazi era, Europeans weren't the only ones who ended up in concentration and slave-labor camps. Americans were also sent there. What's more, the US government knew but decided to take no action.

This untidy bit of history had been hidden for decades. Even with the still-growing mountain of literature on the Holocaust, the fate of Americans has been almost entirely ignored, garnering only a few passing mentions. After stumbling across these shards of an ignored truth, Mitchell G. Bard, PhD, did some serious archival research and conducted fresh interviews, resulting in *Forgotten Victims*, the only book to address the subject.

Bard estimates that "probably a few thousand" US citizens, mainly Jews, spent time in Hitler's camps. Hundreds died there. "American Jews," he explains, "were subject to the same anti-Semitic regulations and dangers as any other Jews who came under control of the Nazis."

Some of the victims were American civilians living in Europe at the wrong time. The State Department sent a total of nine ships during 1939 and 1940 to ferry back Americans living on the Continent. As documents from the time period make clear, State officials believed that Americans who didn't get on those boats deserved whatever happened to them. Around 2,000 of them landed in concentration camps, with at least 200 Jewish Americans ending up in a single one. Small numbers were reported in Dachau and Auschwitz, and some Americans, perhaps dozens, were trapped in the infamous Warsaw ghetto.

Bard further proves that US officials knew *while events were happening* that American citizens were in Nazi camps, prisons, and ghettos, yet they purposely refused to take action. The reasons for this policy of deliberate indifference were varied: These citizens might act as Axis spies. If we act to get American Jews out of harm's way, then *all* Jews will want the same help. Pure pettiness was also to blame: The government seemed miffed that these Americans had chosen to live abroad. In other words, they made their bed; let them die in it.

Captured Allied soldiers were principally kept at POW camps, but several hundred American prisoners of war, some Jewish, were shipped to concentration camps, including Buchenwald, Mauthausen, and the slave labor camp at Berga. Some were summarily executed or worked to death. The US government pled ignorance, but the paper trail shows that at the very least they knew what was happening in Berga. After the war, when the POWs were debriefed, some even giving depositions, the official response was reprehensible. "The government denied many of these atrocities took place," Bard notes, "resisted compensating them for their injuries and failed to bring the perpetrators to justice." ⌷

71
THE US HAS ALMOST NUKED CANADA, BRITAIN, SPAIN, GREENLAND, AND TEXAS

While giving lots of interviews for the release of the first volume of *50 Things*, by far the most popular topic was the accidental nuclear bombing of North Carolina in 1961. It struck such a nerve that a follow-up is more than warranted. The Tar Heel State incident, it turns out, wasn't the first or last time that the US almost accidentally turned a friendly city into the new Hiroshima.

The first such mishap occurred over Canada. On February 13, 1950, a B-36 from Alaska iced up while flying over Vancouver. Before bailing out, the crew veered over the Pacific and dropped their nuclear bomb right off the coast. The conventional explosives detonated, but luckily they didn't trigger a nuclear reaction.

The Royal Air Force Station Lakenheath, around 80 miles from London, was the site of a close call on July 26, 1956. A number of US planes were housed at the base for strategic reasons. One of them, a B-47, crashed and burned while attempting to land. It skidded into a storage building housing three atomic bombs, its blazing fuel setting everything on fire. Each bomb was loaded with four tons of TNT, but the fire was put out before the Mark VI's became dirty bombs.

A telex from the General in charge, declassified decades later, said: "Preliminary exam by bomb disposal officer says a miracle that one Mark Six with exposed detonators didn't go off." When the incident finally came to light, a retired Air Force Major General told a reporter: "It is possible that a part of Eastern England would have become a desert."

A B-47 caught fire and crashed during takeoff in Texas on November 4, 1958. Again, the explosives on the nuke went kaboom, but there was no mushroom cloud explosion.

Spain was the site of the worst such disaster. While refueling over the coastal village of Palomares on January 17, 1966, two planes collided and blew up. The B-52 was carrying four nuclear weapons. One landed safely near the village; another was lost at sea. Three months later, it was fished out of 2,850 feet of water. "The search took about eighty days and employed 3,000 Navy personnel and 33 Navy vessels," according to the Center for Defense Information, "not including ships, planes, and people used to move equipment to the site." The other two A-bombs landed in fields, their explosives went off, and 558 acres were contaminated with plutonium. As part of its contrition, the US military packed 1,400 tons of radioactive dirt into steel drums, then shipped the glowing mess back to the States for disposal. To this day, the Department of Energy still monitors the health of the people and the land.

Two years later (January 21, 1968), a B-52 headed toward Thule US Air Force Base in Greenland crashed seven miles away. Three of the four nukes on board exploded, spritzing plutonium over a large area. In a replay of the Palomares aftermath, 237,000 cubic feet of snow, ice, and debris were packed into drums and freighted to the US for disposal. The evidence conflicts over whether the fourth bomb, which went into the ocean, was recovered or is still underwater.

And this isn't even close to the whole list. There have been many other close calls — crashes of nuke-bearing planes in Kentucky, New Mexico, and Morocco; the jettisoning of two A-bombs off the Delaware coast (never recovered) and one near Tybee Island, Georgia (also never recovered). Then there are the nuclear oopsie-daisies committed by Britain and the Soviet Union. It seems likely that every nuclear power — including France and Israel — must've had similar nail-biting moments, though they've been kept hush-hush.

72
DURING THE COLD WAR, THE CODE TO UNLOCK NUCLEAR MISSILES WAS "00000000"

Missiles being moved around may have presented a few Maalox moments, but when they were in the silos, they were safe and secure, right? You're not gonna launch these babies without bunches of people going through bunches of complicated steps, especially once Defense Secretary Robert McNamara put technical locks on the Minutemen nukes around 1961. Except that the Strategic Air Command thought the eight-digit combinations necessary to launch intercontinental ballistic missiles were for candy-asses, the kind of fraidy-cats who engage the safety on their personal firearms. So the combination for all the missiles was kept at "00000000."

This was revealed by Bruce G. Blair, PhD, who was a Minuteman launch officer during this period. Now the head of the Center for Defense Information, he says: "Our launch checklist in fact instructed us, the firing crew, to double-check the locking panel in our underground launch bunker to ensure that no digits other than zero had been inadvertently dialed into the panel."

When Blair told McNamara about this in 2004, the old warmonger went ballistic. "I am shocked, absolutely shocked and outraged," he blustered. "Who the hell authorized that?"

The locks were finally given legitimate combinations in 1977. ⌗

73
THE GOVERNMENT PRACTICALLY GIVES AWAY VALUABLE LAND TO CORPORATE INTERESTS

It stands to reason that land loaded with gold, silver, platinum, palladium, and other prized minerals would command huge prices. But, as with so many other things, reason has nothing to do with it. The government sells the rights to mine public land for amounts that a schoolkid could buy with allowance money.

It happens under the 1872 Mining Law, which set the prices for mineral rights. Unfortunately, nobody has updated the amounts in the intervening 130+ years, which means that we're stuck with a ridiculous situation.

Just how ridiculous? The Environmental Working Group spent a year gathering data and crunching numbers on the mineral rights to public land in the eleven westernmost states of the continental US, plus Montana.

Depending on how many acres are at issue, you can snatch the mineral rights to public land for

84 cents to $6.75 per acre, with a yearly renewal fee of 52 cents to $5 an acre.

Since 1992, Congress has tacked on an additional $100 annual renewal fee per tract of land (not per acre), but even this token effort is a stop-gap measure. They have yet to make it permanent.

Just to make things even more absurd, it's been possible to outright *buy* the public land, not just the right to mine it, for a little more: $4.06 to $17.10 per acre, depending on total number of acres and the type of mining you want to do. Each year since 1994, Congress has passed an annual moratorium on the ability to purchase land this way, but it refuses to permanently ban the practice.

When the Working Group published its report in 2004, the mining rights for almost 5,570,000 acres of public land had been claimed this way. On top of that, an additional 3,718,000 acres had been flat-out purchased through this form of legalized theft. All told, these lands are controlled by over 26,000 individuals, 2,270 US companies, and 94 foreign companies. (These non-US corporations own over one-fifth of the claimed lands.) As in most things economic, concentration rears its head: "Ten companies and individuals control 21 percent of claimed lands on US public lands," says the EWG.

The owners of the mineral rights and/or the land itself have to plunk down only the nominal fees listed above; they pay the US nothing based on the value of the minerals they mine (in other words, no "royalties" like those rendered by coal, gas, and oil companies). Theoretically, the government could at least see some money based on taxes of the resulting corporate profits, but since the majority of corporations don't pay income tax, this revenue stream is nothing more than a trickle.

As the icing on this demented cake, the government (read: taxpayers) ends up footing the bill for dealing with the pollution and devastation caused by the private mining of these so-called public lands. The mining of metal requires a tiny 0.36 percent of all "industrial facilities," yet it accounts for 46 percent of all industrial pollution.

The Working Group points out some ludicrous real-life examples of the 1872 Mining Law in action:

Land in Crested Butte, Colorado — a ski resort town — goes for a million dollars per acre. The government sold land nearby for $5.64 an acre. The mining company that bought the primo real estate for pocket money estimated that it would net $158 million over the next eleven years.

The Canadian corporation Barrick Gold paid a measly $10,000 for 1,800 acres of Nevada containing an estimated 17.5 million ounces of gold. Bruce Babbit, then Secretary of the Interior, resisted the sale until forced by a court order to proceed. He summed up: "What I'm wondering is why I'm giving $10 billion of the...assets owned by American citizens to a company that's not even an American company?"

A joint mining venture of Chevron and Stillwater Mining Company scored an even bigger take. For their $10,000, they outright bought 1,800 acres of national forest in Montana. As the Working Group points out, they "gained platinum and palladium reserves worth more than $35 billion, a return of $3.5 million for every one dollar received by the federal government."

In some cases, individuals have grabbed public land for a pittance, then sold it for a fortune. One case involves Yucca Mountain, which will soon be home to the nuclear waste of the entire country. When the location of this toxic super-storage facility was announced, some person hotfooted it to the appropriate government office and laid claim to some of the land. Instead of holding onto it to block the plans for an atomic waste dump, he forced the government to pay $250,000 to get back its land.

As noted above, Congress passes temporary measures to make the law's application less ridiculous, but they're too beholden to powerful corporate interests to do anything forceful and lasting. ♂

74
MOST CORPORATIONS PAY
NO FEDERAL INCOME TAX

The fact that most corporations in the US don't pay federal income tax is one of those things that all of us have heard, but we're not sure just how true it is. It's completely true, and now we have the exact figures from the pro-business *Wall Street Journal* and the famously neutral General Accounting Office (an investigative arm of Congress now known as the Government Accountability Office).

The GAO examined millions of tax returns from 1996 through 2000, the economic boom years. They found that 61 percent of

US-based corporations paid no income tax. For foreign-controlled corporations that operate in the US, 71 percent didn't pay.

When they looked strictly at "large" corporations — "those with assets of at least $250 million or gross receipts of at least $50 million in constant 2000 dollars" — the percentages are switched, with 71 percent of large US corporations and 61 percent of large foreign-controlled businesses not contributing to the country's coffers.

To make it even more sickening, most of the corporations that actually do owe taxes pay a rate less than 5 percent, even though the base rate for corporate entities is 35 percent. (Only 0.6 percent of US corporations and 0.1 percent of non-US corporations paid 30 percent or more, the suckers.)

So when you add the corporations that pay no taxes with those that pay tiny taxes, 94 percent of US-controlled companies and 89 percent of foreign-controlled companies paid zero to 4 percent in taxes.

To make sure these numbers weren't due to small businesses that broke even or went belly-up, the bean counters looked at the stats for large corporations only. In this category, 82 percent of US-controlled companies and 76 percent of foreign-controlled companies paid less than 5 percent in taxes.

This failure to pony up their fair share is killing the government's bottom line. The *WSJ* reports:

Corporate tax receipts have shrunk markedly as a share of overall federal revenue in recent years, and were particularly depressed when the economy soured. By 2003, they had fallen to just 7.4% of overall federal receipts, the lowest rate since 1983, and the second-lowest rate since 1934, federal budget officials say. ▢

75
THE MILITARY USED TO PUT SLANDEROUS SECRET CODES ON DISCHARGE PAPERS

When you're discharged from the US military, your personnel file contains a form DD-214, "Report of Separation." It summarizes your service and shows what type of discharge you received. For decades, it secretly revealed much more than that.

Starting in 1947, the US military put a Separation Program Number (SPN) — typically three or four digits, letters, or a combination — on this final piece of paperwork. Unbeknownst to the veterans, this cryptic code revealed *exactly* why they had left the armed forces.

Some of the 500+ codes, especially those developed at the outset, aren't damaging or problematic. They simply indicate run-of-the-mill reasons for leaving the service. For example, "201" means that an enlisted person's term of service ended; "RE-3S" shows that the vet was a family's only surviving son; and "627" indicates that the vet hit the upper age limit and was let go. Most codes, though, are very invasive of privacy. Here are the meanings of some SPN codes:

...YOU'RE NOT
SUPPOSED TO KNOW

- admission of homosexuality or bisexuality • alcoholism • anti-social • AWOL, desertion
- bedwetter • criminalism • discreditable incidents - civilian or military • drug use
- failure of selection for promotion • financial irresponsibility • indebtedness
- interest of national security • obesity • pregnancy • resignation of enlisted personnel on unspecified enlistment in lieu of separation for disloyalty or subversion • schizoid personality
- security reason • separation for concealment of serious arrest record
- sexual deviate • sexual perversion • shirking • unfitness: homosexual acts
- unsanitary habits • withdrawal of ecclesiastical endorsement

Who decided what code to assign, which scarlet letter would follow a vet for the rest of his or her life? In most cases, it was the service member's commanding officer, who had a free hand in the matter. The SPNs weren't given only to people who got dishonorable or other-than-honorable discharges — they were affixed to everyone's record, even those who received honorable or general discharges.

When the existence and purpose of SPNs were officially admitted in 1973, it was further revealed that many employers were well aware of what each code meant. Job applicants who were vets had to make their DD-214's available to potential employers, who would then ask the Pentagon or look up the codes in lists that had been published in obscure, unclassified military documents.

SPNs were vanquished in 1974, due to pressure from Democratic Congressmen. However, vets discharged during the SPN period will still have this marker on their DD-214 unless they specifically request that the military reissue their separation report without the ratfink code. ♡

76
ONE IN THREE AMERICAN HOMELESS MEN IS A MILITARY VETERAN

The US Department of Veterans Affairs reveals: "On any given day, as many as 250,000 veterans (male and female) are living on the streets or in shelters, and perhaps twice as many experience homelessness at some point during the course of a year." That's an awful lot, and the situation is even bleaker when you look at the percentages.

Veterans comprise 6 percent of the overall population, but they're 23 percent of the homeless. Of all homeless men, one-third are vets.

Forty-six percent of homeless vets are 45 or older, compared to 20 percent of the civilian homeless.

The VA says that "the number of homeless male and female Vietnam era veterans is greater than the number of service persons who died during that war."

Though almost half of homeless vets (47 percent) served during 'Nam, they've also served in WWII and every war since, not to mention during peacetime. The National Coalition for Homeless Veterans cites federal figures: "More than 67% served our country for at least three years and 33% were stationed in a war zone."

Peter Dougherty, Director of Homeless Veterans Programs at the VA, candidly told the *Los*

Angeles Times: "Traditionally, what happens to you after you leave has not been a concern of [the] service."

To give some credit, the VA and Defense Department are doing a little to change that, but they still reach only 20 to 25 percent of homeless vets. Many nonprofits are trying to fill the gap, from the above-mentioned National Coalition for Homeless Veterans to local efforts, such as the New England Shelter for Homeless Veterans in Boston. ⌁

77
THE US IMPRISONS MORE OF ITS POPULATION THAN ANY OTHER COUNTRY

The United States is home to almost 5 percent of the world's population, yet it holds 22 percent of the world's prisoners.

The latest official statistics show that as of the middle of 2003, federal, state, and local facilities in America were holding 2,078,570 people.

If we add those on parole or probation, the figure jumps to 6.9 million.

For the last 30 years, the number of prisoners has increased annually. The incarcerated population in mid-2003 is a 2.9 percent rise over the prior year. Currently, one of every 75 men is in the clink.

Not only are the absolute numbers sky-high and ever-increasing, but the rate of imprisonment keeps climbing into higher nosebleed territory, too. In mid-2003, the US imprisoned 709 people out of every 100,000. A year and a half earlier, that figure was 686.

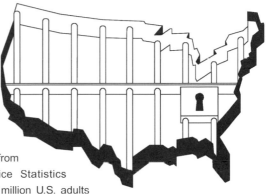

In its mammoth survey of imprisonment from 1974 to 2001, the Bureau of Justice Statistics concluded: "At yearend 2001, over 5.6 million U.S. adults had ever served time in State or Federal prison. If incarceration rates remain unchanged, 6.6% of U.S. residents born in 2001 will go to prison at some time during their lifetime."

These numbers are not only the highest among industrialized nations, they're the highest in the world. The British government's definitive study "World Prison Population List" (fourth edition, 2003) gives the following top five prison nations as of the start of 2002:

US: 686 inmates per 100,000 people
Cayman Islands: 664 • Russia: 638 • Belarus: 554 • Kazakhstan: 522

In Cuba, the rate is approximately 297. Meanwhile, in lovely Iran, the incarceration rate is 229. The US's northern neighbor has a rate of 102, while South of the border, it's 156. England and

Wales combined have a rate of 139. The figures are even lower in Scotland (126) and Northern Ireland (62). The rates for other nations that are interesting for comparison purposes:

Ukraine: 406 • South Africa: 404 • Israel: 153 • Spain: 126 • Australia: 116 • China: 111
Saudi Arabia: 110 • Germany: 96 • Italy: 95 • Uganda: 91 • France: 85 • Vietnam: 71
Japan: 48 • Nigeria: 34 • India: 28

So why does the US keep record numbers of its people in cages? The field of criminal justice is wrestling with that question, and the answers are complicated, but among the biggest factors are an ever-increasing number of laws, mandatory sentencing, and the so-called War on Drugs (drug offenders make up around half the federal prison population). ♡

78
THE GOVERNMENT CAN TAKE YOUR PROPERTY WITHOUT EVEN CHARGING YOU WITH A CRIME

If law enforcement officials even suspect that you're involved in a crime, usually a drug-related one, they can seize your property and keep it. You don't have to be convicted of the crime. In fact, you don't even have to be *charged* with one.

This despotic power, known as asset forfeiture, is widely known (and decried) in many alternative circles, but it has yet to seep into the mainstream consciousness. That's too bad, because it's not a fringe issue but something that has the potential to affect any of us, no matter how law-abiding.

The most likely way an innocent person will get snared in this nightmare is by living with someone — a family member, significant other, or roommate — who's involved with drugs. This is what happened in Albuquerque, New Mexico, in March 2004. Police raided a home occupied by two men, one allegedly involved in the drug trade, the other not. The police busted open a safe in the innocent guy's room, took the $10,000 cash he had received because of a car accident, and kept it. He's suing to get it back.

A month earlier, the *St. Petersburg Times* reported the case of a woman whose acquaintance had stashed a pound of pot in her car without her knowledge. The cops told her that if she signed over her ride, they wouldn't prosecute her. Scared to death, she agreed. When the media started questioning the police about this, they gave back the car. The woman's lawyer said: "This is like a mob shakedown."

Sometimes it's pretty obvious that the property really was knowingly used in commission of crimes. The Border Patrol seizes hundreds upon hundreds of vehicles apparently being used to smuggle people from Mexico into the US. But even in these cases, seizure is a blatantly unconstitutional violation of due process rights. The officers become judge, jury, and executioner.

Federal, state, and local law enforcement agencies all have their own forfeiture programs. At the top level, the Justice Department and the Treasury Department handle this legalized theft. In a report to Congress, Justice tallied the amount of money, real estate, vehicles, art, and other possessions that were "forfeited" in fiscal year 2003: $466,968,207 worth. The Treasury sets its total for the same year at $687,761,000. Well over a billion dollars in one year, and that's just at the federal level.

The Justice Department's website explains the three types of forfeiture. Criminal forfeiture involves a jury and a judge; it's used in the criminal prosecution of individuals and is the hardest form to abuse. In civil judicial forfeiture, a court is also involved but, as Justice explains, "no criminal charge against the owner is necessary." Finally, we have administrative forfeiture, the most egregious variety, in which the feds just snatch people's property. In the words of the Justice Department, it "permits the federal seizing agency to forfeit the property *without judicial involvement.*" It's then up to you to prove that your possessions were wrongly taken.

The practice has its roots in the admiralty laws of England, then America, which hold that inanimate objects can be considered guilty of crimes. The US Supreme Court has upheld this silliness since 1796, and numerous laws from the 1970s and 1980s — such as the RICO conspiracy statutes — only strengthened the practice. The website of the US Marshals Service notes the existence of "more than 200 federal laws that have forfeiture provisions." The Civil Asset Forfeiture Reform Act of 2000 has helped curb the most wanton abuses, though the practice continues. ⛫

79
THE EPA LIED ABOUT NEW YORK'S AIR QUALITY AFTER 9/11

When the Twin Towers of the World Trade Center collapsed on 9/11, humongous plumes of concrete dust, asbestos, lead, and other material hovered over Manhattan. Fires at the site burned for over two months, releasing even more junk, like dioxins, PCBs, and volatile organic compounds.

Yet the Environmental Protection Agency painted a rosy picture of air quality. On September 13, 2001, an EPA press release cheerily said that the results of their testing were "very reassuring" and "uniformly acceptable." Administrator Christine Todd Whitman was quoted: "EPA is greatly relieved to have learned that there appears to be no significant levels of asbestos dust in the air in New York City."

The next day, the EPA's missive soothed frazzled nerves: "EPA continues to believe that there is no significant health risk to the general public in the coming days." On the 18th of that month, Whitman declared: "I am glad to reassure the people of New York and Washington, D.C. that their air is safe to breathe..."

It was all a lie.

The first revelation came in the form of a report from the EPA's Inspector General. The internal watchdog said that at the time the EPA made these pronouncements, it simply didn't have enough data to know whether or not the air was kosher. Of the fourteen toxic substances believed to present the most danger, the EPA didn't have results for ten of them until a week or more after the attacks (that is, after the statement that the "air is safe"). Of the ones it did have, the EPA used imprecise testing methods and incorrect benchmarks.

The report also revealed that the White House had pressured the agency into making its calming claims and had ordered the removal of some precautionary statements, despite the health risks to the public. Additionally, the EPA press releases had to be cleared by the National Security Council before being disseminated.

A leaked memo by Cate Jenkins, PhD, a scientist in the EPA's Office of Solid Waste, exposes additional layers of deceit. She shows that on 9/11 and afterward, tests by the EPA, Con Edison, and others did indeed show that asbestos levels were leaps and bounds above 0.1 percent (the level which EPA considers problematic, requiring action). A level of 4.49 percent was found two blocks from Ground Zero the day after the attacks. On 9/16 and 9/17, at a location sixteen blocks away, tests found a level of 3 percent. One block north, almost two weeks after the attacks, tests measured a whopping 5 percent. All the talk of "reassuring," "acceptable," and "safe" levels was hogwash, and the agency knew it.

Jenkins also reveals: "EPA dismissed levels of toxins such as dioxins as being 'very low' or 'below the detection limit' despite the fact that levels of dioxin measured in the air many blocks away from Ground Zero were the highest ever detected in outdoor air."

The EPA told NY residents that not only didn't they need professional cleaning of their homes and offices, they could clean up the dust, laden with asbestos and other toxins, *on their own* with mops and wet rags. People didn't even need to wear dust masks while doing this. Yet, at the exact same time the EPA was broadcasting these suicidal instructions, the agency had its Manhattan office building professionally cleansed of asbestos. (Not only that, the EPA employed a sensitive, high-tech method to test for asbestos in its building, while it used only an older, less sensitive method for the rest of Manhattan. To add another insult to the mix, the EPA gave its employees gasmasks to use inside its building, while assuring everyone else that they didn't even need the cheap painters masks you can buy at hardware stores.)

Further actions on the part of the EPA are just as inexplicably callous. In 1998, when one floor of a federal building in Manhattan was contaminated with asbestos from insulation, the EPA tested 4,000 to 5,000 samples *on that floor alone*. How many samples did it test in all of Manhattan after 9/11? Around 250.

And some people still crinkle their brows, unable to comprehend why so many of us don't trust the government.... ▢

80
CONDOLEEZZA RICE COMMITTED PERJURY BEFORE THE 9/11 COMMISSION

During her April 8, 2004, appearance before the 9/11 Commission, National Security Adviser Condoleezza Rice discussed the infamous Presidential Daily Brief of August 6, 2001. At the time, the document was still classified. We did, however, know the title: "Bin Ladin Determined to Strike In US."

Rice was asked by commission member Richard Ben-Veniste: "Isn't it a fact, Dr. Rice, that the August 6 PDB warned against possible attacks in this country?"

Keeping in mind that Rice was under oath, read her reply:

"You said, did it not warn of attacks. It did not warn of attacks inside the United States. It was historical information based on old reporting. There was no new

threat information. And it did not, in fact, warn of any coming attacks inside the United States."

In the continuing testy exchange, she reiterated: "Commissioner, this was not a warning. This was a historic memo…"

Then she gets specific about how nonspecific the memo was: "But I can also tell you that there was nothing in this memo that suggested that an attack was coming on New York or Washington, D.C."

So here we have the President's top adviser on security swearing before God and country that the memo "Bin Ladin Determined to Strike In US" did not discuss Bin Laden's plans to strike in the US.

It seemed absolutely ridiculous, but we had to take her word for it. Not for long, though. Two days later — under intense pressure — the White House miraculously released the document, 99 percent uncensored. Some of the short memo did discuss the past (this was the "historical information" part) but only as a way of emphasizing Bin Laden's continuing willingness to attack America. The briefing says that this illustrates his patience, his tactic of planning strikes for years. His earlier plots were just the first part of his plans to attack inside the US itself, the memo warns. In bold italics, it blares: "Al-Qa'ida members — including some who are US citizens — have resided in or traveled to the US for years, and the group apparently maintains a support structure that could aid attacks."

This all builds up to the crescendo of the last two paragraphs, which explicitly warn that plots are underway:

... FBI information since that time indicates patterns of suspicious activity in this country consistent with preparations for hijacking or other types of attacks, including recent surveillance of federal buildings in New York.

The FBI is conducting approximately 70 full field investigations throughout the US that it considers Bin Ladin-related. CIA and the FBI are investigating a call to our Embassy in the UAE [United Arab Emirates] in May saying that a group of Bin Ladin supporters was in the US planning attacks with explosives.

This is the "historical" memo that contained "no new threat information." The briefing that "did not warn of attacks inside the United States," certainly not anything about an attack on New York.

When mere mortals lie under oath, it's called perjury. When National Security Advisers lie under oath to Congressionally-mandated commissions, it's called…nothing, really. Because no one mentions it.

It's worth noting that Bush also lied about the warning memo, claiming that the "PDB said nothing about an attack on America." ⌕

81
AL QAEDA ATTACKS HAVE INCREASED SUBSTANTIALLY SINCE 9/11

Despite the very costly "War on Terror" — which, we are repeatedly assured, is making the world safer than ever before — attacks by al Qaeda have skyrocketed. This supposedly "decimated" network of terrorists has been busier, and more deadly, than ever *after* the attacks of September 11, 2001.

The famously neutral, thorough Congressional Research Service — whose reports are almost never made available to the general public — looked at the number of al Qaeda attacks perpetrated in the two and a half years after 9/11, balanced against the number of attacks during that amount of time before 9/11.

While some experts believe that there's no such thing as "al Qaeda," that the term was created by the CIA to refer to groups, cells, and individuals that have little, if anything, to do with each other, the CRS looked at incidents that the government credits to al Qaeda. Thus, under the establishment's own rules of the game, al Qaeda's attacks went from *one* in the 30 months before 9/11, to *ten* during the 30 months after 9/11.

The discrepancy is even worse when you look at the number of fatalities. Before 9/11: 17 deaths. After 9/11: 510 deaths.

When comparing injuries, the difference becomes 64-fold. In the 30 months before 9/11, al Qaeda injured 39 people. In the 30 months after, it injured 2,526.

The differences can be considered even more lopsided because the one pre-9/11 attack was the bombing of the *USS Cole* in Yemen. The report explains that "some experts do not include this attack as a 'terrorist incident,' because it was directed against a military, not civilian, target, although the Cole was not engaged in combat during that period." One of the post-9/11 attacks was against military personnel in Kuwait. So if we take out the two military attacks, the scorecard is zero to nine.

Even if we lengthen the time period to look at *all* al Qaeda attacks prior to 9/11, the news is still bad. Al Qaeda's first attack took place in December 1992. During the almost nine years until 9/11, there were four attacks, two of which were against military targets: the *Cole* and US servicemen in Somalia.

So, the final tally:

Two attacks against civilian targets and two against military targets in the nine years prior to 9/11.

Nine attacks against civilian targets and one against a military target in the two and a half years after 9/11. ⛝

82
THE PATRIOT ACT IS USED IN CASES THAT HAVE NOTHING TO DO WITH TERRORISM

We were assured that the USA Patriot Act would be wielded only to nab terrorists. After all, in the law's full, convoluted name — Uniting and Strengthening America by Providing Appropriate Tools Required to Intercept and Obstruct Terrorism Act — the *only* crime mentioned is terrorism. According to US Representative Ron Paul (R-TX), Congress, shaken by 9/11, didn't even read the gargantuan bill before passing it. They apparently bought the line that it was necessary to prevent more attacks and voted for it sight unseen.

Attorney General John Ashcroft, in defending the act — which he frequently has to do — only mentions its role in terrorism. In his speeches about it, he says the following (or something almost exactly like it):

"The Patriot Act does three things: First, it closes the gaping holes in our ability to investigate *terrorists*. Second, the Patriot Act updates our *anti-terrorism* laws to meet the challenges of new technology, and new threats. Third, the Patriot Act has allowed us to build an extensive team that shares information and fights *terrorism* together."

In another speech, he invoked 9/11: "Armed with the tools provided by the Patriot Act, the men and women of justice and law enforcement have dedicated themselves to the unfinished work of those who resisted, those who assisted, and those who sacrificed on September 11th."

He told Congress: "Our ability to prevent another catastrophic attack on American soil would be more difficult, if not impossible, without the Patriot Act. It has been the key weapon used across America in successful counter-terrorist operations to protect innocent Americans from the deadly plans of terrorists."

When he signed the legislation into law, President Bush said: "These terrorists must be pursued, they must be defeated, and they must be brought to justice. And that is the purpose of this legislation."

Get it? It's all about terrorism. In all of their speeches and public comments, Ashcroft and Bush never even faintly whispered about any other use of the Patriot Act. But those other uses have been legion.

Around two years after 9/11, unnamed Justice Department officials admitted that the act has been applied in "hundreds" of cases that had nothing to do with terrorism.

The Patriot Act was used to investigate allegations that an owner of two Las Vegas titty clubs was bribing local officials. The feds invoked section 314 of the act to get financial records of the parties under suspicion. That particular part of the act applies to people suspected "of engaging in terrorist acts or money laundering activities." Notice the weasel-word "or." They can be engaged in terrorism *or* they can be laundering money for any purpose under the Sun.

Section 319 of the law was used to get money from a lawyer indicted on charges of bilking his clients. He skipped the country and allegedly put a wad of cash in Belizean banks. When Belize refused to turn over the dough, the feds invoked the Patriot Act to seize $1.7 million from the banks' accounts in the US.

The owner of a fan website devoted to the sci-fi show *Stargate SG-1* posted streaming video of episodes for download. MGM and the Motion Picture Association of America called in the FBI for this alleged copyright violation, and they whipped out the Patriot Act to get the webmaster's financial records from his ISP.

From January through October 2003, a computer science grad student in Madison, Wisconsin, disrupted emergency radio frequencies over a several block radius. One of his feats was to broadcast X-rated recordings over police radios. The student was considered intellectually gifted but socially retarded, and even the US Assistant Attorney who prosecuted the case said that the "immaturity of the defendant" was the motivator, not terrorism. Nonetheless, prosecuted under section 814 of the Patriot Act, which covers "cyberterrorism," the radio hacker got eight years in the slammer.

A Mexican citizen who pled guilty to attempting to smuggle over $824,000 from Alabama to his home country was nailed under a Patriot Act provision covering the reporting of currency.

The expanded surveillance capabilities of the act were also used to break up two rings of child pornographers/molesters, to track down a man who had abducted and sexually assaulted his estranged wife, and to break up an ecstasy-smuggling operation.

Additionally, the Justice Department has exploited the Patriot Act to:

- bust scammers who steal credit card info over the Net;
- find a woman who had been kidnapped;
- pinch a hacker who stole a company's trade secrets.

Further, the *New York Times* reported: "Authorities also have used their expanded authority to track private Internet communications in order to investigate a major drug distributor, a four-time killer, an identity thief and a fugitive who fled on the eve of trial by using a fake passport."

Just give us these powers, the authorities said, and we'll only use them to nail evil-doing terrorists, to avenge those killed on 9/11, to keep Ma and Pa Kettle safe from the brown hordes of al Qaeda. But now these expanded powers are being against hackers, bribers, copyright violators, con artists, kidnappers, killers, child pornographers, cash smugglers, ecstasy makers, and radio jammers. And that's just what's we know about.

Not that the end result of busting some of these characters is a bad thing in and of itself. But if these new powers of law enforcement are so wonderful and necessary and legitimate, why were they sold to us solely as anti-terrorism measures? Why has the Administration refused to acknowledge that the Patriot Act is being used against myriad crimes, from low-level stuff to serious violations?

Rest assured, this power grab was meant from the beginning to apply across the board. After all, most provisions of the Patriot Act had been written well before 9/11, but they couldn't get passed due to Congress-critters who were concerned about that quaint relic called the US Constitution. These blocked measures just needed the perfect excuse to become law. Along came 9/11... ⬚

83
THE GOVERNMENT OFFERED AROUND 30 REASONS FOR THE IRAQ INVASION

Just why did the US need to invade a militarily powerless Third World country on the other side of the globe? What could convince Americans to part with hundreds of billions of dollars and to send their sons and daughters to be killed, blinded, and mutilated? Obviously, just one reason wasn't going to do it. Neither would two or three. So the government, primarily members of the Bush Administration itself, trotted out around *30* reasons to invade and occupy an undeveloped country, kill and injure tens of thousands of civilians, and throw gasoline on the fire of jihadists, while sacrificing lives, limbs, and money.

We know the big three:

• Because Iraq possessed biological and chemical weapons, which the US had sold to Saddam in the 1980s and which Saddam destroyed in the late 1990s. Well in advance of the invasion, chief UN weapons inspector Hans Blix plainly stated that the WMD were gone. After the war, chief US weapons inspector David Kay — a Republican hand-picked by the Bushies to find the WMD — also declared that the stockpiles don't exist. He said that anyone who clings to the notion of their existence is "really delusional," also telling reporters: "I think it's most important that the president of the United States recognizes that in fact the weapons are not there."

• Because Iraq supported al Qaeda, even though no evidence of this connection has ever been found and, in a virtually ignored press conference, Bush flat-out admitted that Iraq was not involved in 9/11. (Tony Blair, at the conference with Bush, immediately backed him up on this point. Powell admitted the same thing in February 2002.) In summer 2004, the 9/11 Commission and the Senate Select Committee on Intelligence put what should be the final nails in the coffin, each body issuing a report bluntly declaring that there has never been a working relationship between Saddam and al Qaeda. Meanwhile, terrorist-supporting states such as Pakistan are considered America's great friends.

• Because Saddam was a dictator who oppressed the Iraqi people. This is true, but let's not forget that the Administration expresses no interest in "liberating" oppressed people in dozens of other tyrannies, such as Cuba, Burma, the Democratic Republic of Congo, China, Swaziland, and Sudan. Now that the WMD have proven to be vaporware, and the Iraq/Qaeda connection has been shot down, this "for the Iraqi people" excuse has retroactively become the dominant one. But even megahawk Paul Wolfowitz, the Deputy Secretary of Defense, has stated that this "by itself, as I think I said earlier, is a reason to help the Iraqis but it's not a reason to put American kids' lives at risk, certainly not on the scale we did it."

Aside from the big three, all inoperative, over two dozen other justifications popped up. The list below contains many — but not all — of the justifications that University of Illinois student Devon M. Largio scrupulously documented in her headline-making political science thesis on this topic:

• Whether or not Saddam had WMD, he *wanted* them.
• Iraq may have been involved in the anthrax mailings right after 9/11.
• The US should've deposed Saddam during the 1991 Gulf War.
• Iraq is weak and could be easily trounced.

- Iraq is a danger to the entire world and everyone in the world.
- Iraq is a threat specifically to the US.
- Iraq is a danger mainly to its neighbors.
- Iraq hasn't upheld UN resolutions.
- Saddam Hussein is an evil man.
- Attacking Iraq would spread democracy and capitalism throughout the Middle East.
- We don't know what Iraq's intentions are.
- It would send a message to other countries about aiding terrorists.
- For the sake of children in the US and the world.
- Invading Iraq would lead to world peace.
- Iraq was trying to get or develop nuclear weapons.
- Iraq must be invaded in order to defend freedom.
- Saddam Hussein was violating international law (by developing WMD).
- Because of the way history will judge us.
- Because Saddam hates the US.

As hard as it is to believe, the well of reasons hasn't yet run dry. When drumming up support for the Iraq attack, Bush twice mentioned that Hussein had allegedly tried to assassinate the first President Bush in April 1993. At a political fundraiser in Houston, late in September 2002, Bush said: "After all, this is the guy who tried to kill my dad." This has struck some observers as the most honest statement explaining Bush's burning desire to smack down Hussein.

Then we have the obvious reason for the war: to gain control of oil. No Cabinet-level member of the Administration said this in public, but President Bush's top economic adviser did.

In September 2002, Lawrence Lindsay enthused to the pro-war *Wall Street Journal*:

"When there is a regime change in Iraq, you could add three million to five million barrels [of oil per day] of production to world supply. The successful prosecution of the war would be good for the economy."

Undersecretary of Commerce Grant Aldonas said much the same thing, that invading Iraq "would open up this spigot on Iraqi oil which certainly would have a profound effect in terms of the performance of the world economy for those countries that are manufacturers and oil consumers."

While debating an energy bill on June 15, 2004, the Chairman of the House Energy and Commerce Committee, Republican Rep. Billy Tauzin, said:

"We are in dire need of a policy that tells the energy future traders on Wall Street to quit running the prices up and to begin thinking about a future where we are producing more energy at home for our own people instead of constantly fighting over battlefields to defend other people's energy supplies that we depend upon."

We mustn't overlook the much-circulated admission by Brigadier General William Looney, head of the US Central Command's Airborne Expeditionary Force. While talking to *Defense Week* about the no-fly zones over Iraq, he said: "It's a good thing, especially when there is a lot of oil out there we need."

And who could forget the "flypaper" rationale? In this bizarre scenario, America went to Iraq in order to draw all terrorists into that one country, where they could be conveniently dispatched, hopefully before blowing up or shooting too many US troops. Apparently, every terrorist in the world booked passage to Iraq, leaving not a single one available to attack Western interests elsewhere. Vice President Cheney was the main proponent of this fantasy, saying things like this on *Meet the Press*:

"So what we do on the ground in Iraq, our capabilities here are being tested in no small measure, but this is the place where we want to take on the terrorists. This is the place where we want to take on those elements that have come against the United States, and it's far more appropriate for us to do it there and far better for us to do it there than it is here at home."

Another reason for the invasion — this one largely unspoken — is the religious aspect: Christians versus infidels. Bush, as most everyone knows, is a hardcore fundamentalist who believes that he is directly doing God's bidding. The war against terror — in which Iraq is supposedly the primary battleground — is actually a holy war, not just to Mullah Omar, but to Bush as well. One indication is his famous use of the loaded word "crusade" to describe the battle.

Another example comes from a Bush cousin. For the widely overlooked book *The Bushes: Portrait of a Dynasty*, a Reagan hagiographer and his wife conducted unprecedented, candid interviews with many members of the Bush clan, leading Doug Wead — a former aide to both Presidents Bush — to remark: "The Schweizers have penetrated to the heart of the Bush family. This is as close as anyone has ever been able to get." A cousin who didn't want to be named opened up about the war on terror:

"George sees this as a religious war. He doesn't have a p.c. view of this war. His view of this is that they are trying to kill the Christians. And we as the Christians will strike back with more force and more ferocity than they will ever know."

Also part of the new crusade is Lt. Gen. William G. "Jerry" Boykin, the Deputy Undersecretary of Defense for Intelligence. When not leading the hunt for bin Laden and other top prizes in the war on terror, Boykin appears in full uniform in front of fundie gatherings and says things like: "We in the army of God, in the house of God, kingdom of God have been raised for such a time as this." When speaking of one of his Muslim adversaries, he thunders: "I knew my God was bigger than his. I knew that my God was a real God and his was an idol."

Another reason that has received almost zero public attention was proffered by Philip Zelikow, who at the time was on the President's Foreign Intelligence Advisory Board. This influential body monitors intelligence agencies — including the CIA, NSA, and Defense Intelligence Agency — and it reports directly to the President. Members have above top-secret security clearance, which allows them access to any classified information. As part of a panel at the University of Virginia on September 10, 2002 — right when the Administration started hard-selling the upcoming invasion — Zelikow said:

"Why would Iraq attack America or use nuclear weapons against us? I'll tell you what I think the real threat [is] and actually has been since 1990: It's the threat against Israel.

"And this is the threat that dare not speak its name, because the Europeans don't care deeply about that threat, I will tell you frankly. And the American government doesn't want to lean too hard on it rhetorically, because it is not a popular sell."

Three leading neoconservative architects of the invasion — Richard Perle, Undersecretary of Defense Douglas Feith, and David Wurmser (now the Vice President's Middle East Adviser) — used to be part of the Study Group on a New Israeli Strategy Toward 2000. In 1996, they released a paper called "A Clean Break: A New Strategy for Securing the Realm," which recommended that Hussein be removed as leader of Iraq, partly because this is "an important Israeli strategic objective in its own right" and partly because it would weaken Syria's ambitions.

Speaking of "selling" the war, a senior Administration figure openly admitted that this approach — attempting to convince Americans that it needed this invasion just like it needs detergent or Twinkies — was the operative one.

In early September 2002, White House Chief of Staff Andrew Card was asked why the Administration was starting to push its Iraq agenda so hard. He replied: "From a marketing point of view, you don't introduce new products in August." ¤

84
A LEADING PENTAGON HAWK ADMITTED THE IRAQ INVASION WAS ILLEGAL

Powerbroker Richard Perle was one of the prime movers behind the 2003 war on Iraq. He'd been pushing for it for more than a decade, since the original Gulf War.

This superhawk, known in the Beltway as the Prince of Darkness, was Reagan's Assistant Secretary of Defense, and he advised the first President Bush on foreign policy. He's heavily involved with two prime outlets of neo-conservative war-mongering — the Project for a New American Century and the American Enterprise Institute.

As the Chair of the influential, un-accountable Defense Policy Board — which advises the Defense Department's leaders — from 2001 to March 2003, he was in a perfect position to push for an Iraq attack. Not only did he have Rumsfeld's ear, he was backed by the number-two and number-three men in the Defense Department — Paul Wolfowitz and Douglas Feith — who for

| ...YOU'RE NOT
SUPPOSED TO KNOW

years had been jonesing to kick Iraq's ass. (Feith is the one who appointed Perle to the board.)

So it was very strange when Perle admitted that the war he fought so hard to start was illegal. Speaking in London at an event for the Institute of Contemporary Arts, he told the audience: "I think in this case international law stood in the way of doing the right thing." He groused that international law "would have required us to leave Saddam Hussein alone," something that Perle and his cohorts couldn't tolerate.

The London *Guardian* explains:

President George Bush has consistently argued that the war was legal either because of existing UN security council resolutions on Iraq — also the British government's publicly stated view — or as an act of self-defence permitted by international law.

But here we have the Pentagon's top adviser, who regularly appeared on TV to bang the drum for war, admitting that the US engaged in an illegal invasion.

As they say in Washington: Laws are for the little people. ⌑

85
THE US RUNS A NETWORK OF
AT LEAST 20 SECRET PRISONS

Not too many things are more antithetical to constitutional and moral principles than secret prisons. Keeping prisoners incommunicado in remote, sometimes undisclosed facilities with no meaningful oversight brings to mind medieval dungeons, Star Chambers, and the Black Hole of Calcutta. Yet 21st century America has set up at least 20 such shadowy facilities. Some are officially admitted to exist, although we have next to no idea of what goes on inside, but authorities won't even concede the existence of some of the others. Both George W. Bush and State Department Coordinator for Counterterrorism Cofer Black have stated that at least 3,000 detainees have entered this subterranean network of off-the-books prisons.

The most well-known no-man's-land is at the Naval Base at Guantanamo Bay, Cuba. Originally, detainees were held in the outdoor Camp X-Ray; then they were moved to Camp Delta, built by Halliburton for an average cost of $47,550 for each 6-by-8-foot cell. The number of people held in this Caribbean gulag is usually given as somewhere around 600.

The other dark hole with the highest visibility is the Abu Ghraib prison near Baghdad, which dominated world headlines for weeks after *60 Minutes II* quit obeying the Pentagon and mustered the courage to broadcast photos of prisoners being beaten, abused, and sexually humiliated by giddy US military personnel.

The final facility with a somewhat high profile is the Collection Center located at the US Air Force

Base in Bagram, Afghanistan, which is said to be the primary detention center in that country. (The CIA has its own off-the-record hellhole in Bagram, plus another one — called The Pit — in Kabul.) Then there's the holding pen at Kandahar, supposedly just a way station for those headed to Bagram to enjoy the Air Force's hospitality. US Central Command has said that Afghanistan has many more facilities, as many as 20, that are just temporary stops on the road to Bagram, either directly or via Kandahar. The number of detainees is reportedly 300-something.

Iraq is home to a bare minimum of twelve detainment facilities run by the US military or the so-called Coalition. In addition to Abu Ghraib, the two big facilities are Camp Cropper and Camp Bucca, with smaller ones scattered about.

The only known Constitution-free detention center on US soil is the Consolidated Naval Brig in Charleston, South Carolina. It's home to two US citizens — José Padilla and Yaser Hamdi — who were held without legal recourse for two years before the Supreme Court half-heartedly stepped into the vicious battle over their fates. The brig also holds Qatar citizen Ali Saleh Kahlah al-Marri, who was originally indicted on fraud and vague terrorism charges through the normal justice process; just before trial, though, Bush declared him an enemy combatant, and he was whisked into the brig.

Numerous news articles focus on detention centers in Pakistan, but US authorities refuse to comment. The neither-confirm-nor-deny approach also holds for a reported CIA vacation spot in Jordan, the Al Jafr prison. On the other hand, the Pentagon specifically denies continued reports of captives being held at the US Naval base on the supremely remote island of Diego Garcia.

Human Rights First, the first group to tally all of these secret prisons, also notes that small numbers of detainees — including "American Taliban" John Walker Lindh — have been held for short periods aboard US warships.

The group points out the Grand Canyon-size gulf between words and deeds: "In its Country Reports on human rights conditions abroad, the US Department of State has consistently criticized the practice of holding individuals incommunicado in secret detention facilities."

86
THE GOVERNMENT HAS A DATABASE OF EVERY CHILD PORN IMAGE EVER MADE

The federal government has created a database that will eventually contain every child pornography image ever created, from those in old Danish magazines to digital photos put online to private pictures seized from busted pervs.

I'm reminded of the (probably) apocryphal tales of the Vatican's secret porn collection, said to be the largest in the world. In this case, though, it's true. The feds are building an all-inclusive archive of kiddie porn, and it's remotely accessible (i.e., people physically located away from the computers housing the database can still log into it).

They've been keeping quiet about such an important plan. The only mentions of the database come in a single paragraph in a press release from the Department of Homeland Security and two paragraphs in a Government Accountability Office report.

The Homeland Security release concerns Operation Predator, a scheme to crack down on child molesters. One part of the plan involves the database, which has been jointly created by the Department of Homeland Security's Bureau of Immigration and Customs Enforcement (which houses the database), the FBI, the Secret Service, the Justice Department's Child Exploitation and Obscenity Section, the Postal Inspection Service, and the National Center for Missing and Exploited Children, with help from law enforcement agencies of other countries. The reasons are explained:

With its capacity to search and identify known images, the system is designed to help law enforcement agencies throughout the world identify and rescue children featured in the images. The system is also designed to facilitate prosecution of those who possess or distribute digital child pornography images in the wake of a 2002 Supreme Court decision (Ashcroft v. Free Speech Coalition) requiring proof that such images depict an actual child.

They say that "this system will eventually contain all known child pornography images."

The GAO report concerns the use of peer-to-peer networks — best known for allowing users to swap unauthorized MP3s of corporate-controlled music — to share child pornography. Toward the end, the publication mentions the kiddie porn archive, confirming that it went live in January 2003, with the goal of the first phase being 100,000 images. It's "being populated with all known and unique child pornographic images obtained from national and international law enforcement sources and from CyberTipline reports filed with NCMEC."

Although housed at Customs, it "can be accessed remotely" by the agencies involved, including the nongovernmental National Center for Missing and Exploited Children.

In some ways, this sounds like a good idea, and the DHS claims that in its first six months, the system identified six kids in roughly 300 images. But putting all of this radioactively illegal, far-flung, extremely hard-to-obtain material into one place protected by just a password raises a whole raft of tough questions. Precisely who at each of these agencies will have access to this cornucopia of kiddie porn? How closely will access be monitored? How tight is the system's security? How often will passwords be changed? What happens if hackers compromise it? What are the implications of allowing a private organization to have access? What kind of oversight will there be? Public oversight has been nil, and by the time Congress was informed by the GAO, the database had already been a *fait accompli* for nine months. Let's hope that NAMBLA (the North American Man/Boy Love Association) doesn't have an accomplished hacker within its ranks. ◻

87
PRESIDENTIAL DEBATES ARE STRICTLY CONTROLLED BY THE TWO MAJOR POLITICAL PARTIES

The great presidential debates of Lincoln-Douglas and Kennedy-Nixon have devolved into a canned photo-op where the candidates mouth platitudes, the same talking points we heard them parrot during the whole interminable campaign.

How did this happen? How did a free-spirited exchange of ideas, with gloves-off sparring between the opponents, become neutered and boring? In 1988, the two major parties realized that the debates were too un-predictable, too likely to harm a candidate. They weren't worth the risk. Something had to be done to turn them into stage-managed press conferences.

The national Republican and Democratic parties teamed up (again proving that they're just two sides of the same worthless coin) and created the Commission on Presidential Debates to control things. Comprised of operatives from both parties and funded by corporations, the CPD runs the show, having given the boot to the independent League of Women Voters.

This puppet on a string does the bidding of the Demopublican machine, virtually assuring that nothing threatening can happen to either major party candidate. As part of that mission, the CPD does everything it can to shut out third-party challengers. The CPD's director stated in 2002: "I think it's obvious that independent candidates mess things up."

Almost every aspect of the debates — where they will be held, who asks the questions, times for responses and rebuttals, whether the candidates may directly engage each other, who'll be in the audience, the height of the podiums — is dictated by the candidates. Representatives of both politicians sign a secret contract that spells out the terms in black and white. The CPD simply carries out these orders.

The nonprofit group Open Debates — which is attempting to put the debates under the control of a citizens' commission — has released leaked copies of these contracts. The 1996 agreement, for the debates between Clinton and Dole (and their veeps), said:

No follow-up questions by the moderator will be permitted, and no cross-questions by the candidates or cross-conversation between the candidates will be allowed under these rules.

Contracts for other years have had the same basic rules, which make for "debates" that are about as enthralling as watching paint dry.

Even the first President Bush admitted (after the fact): "It's too much show business and too much prompting, too much artificiality, and not really debates. They're rehearsed appearances." ▢

88
FOR OVER 100 YEARS, ALMOST EVERY DISCHARGE OF WASTE INTO US WATERS HAS BEEN ILLEGAL

We've all had a laugh over those ridiculous, unenforced laws that are still on the books, like the ones that forbid impersonating a wolf or buying a hat without a spouse's permission. But there are a few extremely important laws still in force that are lying around unused, rusting away from neglect. One of those laws is the Refuse Act, passed in 1899 as part of the Rivers and Harbors Act.

This federal law explicitly outlaws the chucking of refuse into a navigable body of water, which includes oceans, rivers, lakes, even wetlands, as well as the tributaries that feed any of them.

The one and only kind of waste that can be disposed of in this manner is the liquid gunk that already flows through the streets and sewers. If you want to toss *anything* else into the drink, there's only one way to legally do it: Get written permission from the Secretary of the Army, who first must get the nod from the Army Corps of Engineers. Needless to say, if anyone ever did do this, it hasn't been done in many, many decades.

A violation is considered a misdemeanor, the punishment being imprisonment for one to six months and/or a fine of up to $25,000 for each day the pollution occurs.

In 1966, the Supreme Court upheld the Refuse Act, specifying that it applied to industrial waste in addition to any other form of refuse (besides street/sewer runoff). From that time into the early 1970s, the law was brandished against such behemoths as US Steel, DuPont, and Standard Oil.

Then the Clean Water Act became law in 1972, and the legal situation — not to mention the nation's water — got a lot murkier. While the Refuse Act outlawed all dumping sans Army permission, the Clean Water Act tried to set up reasonable amounts, varying by industry, location, type of pollutant, etc. In other words, it gave corporations a whole lot of wiggle room.

In recent years, the Refuse Act has been dusted off and used on extremely rare occasions. In 1991, Exxon pled guilty to violating several laws, including the Refuse Act, for the *Valdez* disaster. The next year, the EPA reports: "Pipeline rupture caused an 860,000 gallon oil spill into the Mississippi, Gasconade, and Missouri rivers. Shell pleaded guilty to violation of the Refuse Act and agreed to pay $8,400,000 in fines, restitution, and settlements." In 1997, a small salvage company and its owner were busted under the Refuse Act and other federal laws for dumping crap into Maryland's Patapsco River.

Maybe the best part is that the statute gives a strong incentive for ordinary citizens to nail polluters. If you turn in a corporation or other entity that's fouling the water, and your information leads to a conviction under the Refuse Act, you get *half* of the fine levied. Even if the government won't pursue the charges, you can bring a case against the polluter in the name of the government in order to collect the dough.

The Refuse Act is still in force and has been blessed by the Supreme Court, so every discharge or dumping of waste without the Army Secretary's permission for over a century has been a federal crime. This includes everything from private boats that spew oil into a lake to broken pipelines, ruptured oil tankers, municipalities that discharge raw sewage, mines that dump fill, factory farms that dispose of animal waste, and, of course, factories and plants that toss the entire periodic table into our water.

The National Resource Defense Council noted in 2002: "Some 218 million Americans live within 10 miles of a polluted lake, river, stream or coastal area. About 45 percent of the nation's assessed waters are still unsafe for fishing, swimming or supporting aquatic life — up from 40 percent in 1998." That's an awful lot of Refuse Act violations. ⌼

89
THE WATER SUPPLY IS FILLED WITH SMALL AMOUNTS OF PHARMACEUTICALS AND OTHER CHEMICALS

Every time you wash your tub with a cleaner, rinse off make-up or suntan lotion, pour coffee down the drain, or flush old prescription drugs, small amounts of their chemical components end up in the water supply. Maybe the most surprising source of pollutants is our own waste. Whenever you go to the bathroom, you're excreting small bits of everything you take — all the prescription and illegal drugs, the caffeine and nicotine, the aspirin and cough medicine. With most of these substances, small portions make it out of your body unaltered or just slightly changed. Don't expect treatment to catch these nasties. The Environmental Protection Agency baldly declares: "No municipal sewage treatment plants are engineered for PPCP removal." ("PPCP" stands for "pharmaceuticals and personal care products.")

The EPA first discovered a pharmaceutical chemical in water in 1976, but the emphasis at the time was on industrial pollutants, so no one paid much attention to it. In the 1980s, Europe started studying this kind of contamination in earnest. The US got in on the act in the mid-1990s, but PPCP pollution is still under the radar. In fact, of the major environmentalism websites I checked, none of them discussed pharmaceuticals and other personal care products in our drinking water.

In 1999 and 2000, the US Geological Survey checked *agua* samples in 30 states, finding 82 types of this class of pollutant (they looked for 95). The median amount was seven, with one stream containing 38. Among the most common were cholesterol, steroids, caffeine, a fire retardant, a disinfectant, and an insect repellant. A 1998 survey of 40 German waterways found 31 drugs and five metabolites. These and other studies in the US, Canada, and Europe have found antibiotics, hormones (mainly from birth control pills), antidepressants, codeine, high blood pressure meds, antacids, ibuprofen, musks, Darvon (a synthetic opioid), nicotine metabolites, blood lipid regulators, and the radioactive stuff you drink before getting X-rayed. No one has yet tested for illegal drugs, but given their rate of use, they and their metabolites have to be part of the mix.

So there's no doubt that our water supply is swimming with microscopic portions of chemicals from dandruff shampoo, Viagra, and pot. The question is what kind of effect this is having on us and on aquatic life. Scientists involved with the issue frankly admit that we just don't know. When it comes to humans, researchers have yet to study in-depth the effects of these micro-doses. As far as fish and other aquatic beasties are concerned, until recently no one thought to study the effects. Who would've thought, as a 2003 study found, that fish in Texas would have Prozac in their brains and livers? Beyond that, the studies that are done look at the effect of just one chemical, but in the real world these chemicals are occurring in combinations, resulting in cocktails with perhaps unknowable effects.

A hydrologist with the US Geological Survey, Sheila Murphy, summed up the problem as pointedly as anyone could: "It doesn't just go down the toilet and into Neverland." ⌂

90
WELL OVER 300,000 TONS OF CHEMICAL WEAPONS HAVE BEEN DUMPED INTO THE SEA

Industrial waste and drugs aren't the only water waste we need to worry about. For decades, the world's oceans were used as a giant garbage can for the most noxious, lethal chemicals in existence. Countries have dumped hundreds of thousands of tons of weapons loaded with cyanide, mustard gas, sarin, phosgene, VX, Zyklon B, and other nerve agents into the drink.

Such dumps started around the time of the first World War, but documentation of this early activity is practically nonexistent. The practice kicked into overdrive in the immediate aftermath of WWII. Faced with huge stockpiles of Germany's weapons, the Allies pitched them into the waters around Europe. NATO officially estimates that from 1945 to 1947, 300,000 tons of these weapons — containing 60,000 tons of nerve agents — were heaved into the Baltic and the North Atlantic.

Japan had much less of this stuff than the Nazis, but still almost 5,000 tons were cast into the Pacific. Britain and Australia used this

...YOU'RE NOT SUPPOSED TO KNOW

method to dispose of some of their own arsenals after hostilities ended. Dumps in the 1950s continued to be primarily of WWII-vintage nerve agents. In the late sixties and 1970, the US jettisoned tens of thousands of its own leaky, sarin-loaded M-55 rockets into the Atlantic.

The *Bulletin of the Atomic Scientists* reports:

In all, the United States is responsible for 60 sea dumpings totaling about 100,000 tons of chemical weapons filled with toxic materials, according to a 1993 study by the US Arms Control and Disarmament Agency (acda). The US sites are located in the Gulf of Mexico, off the coast of New Jersey, California, Florida, [New York] and South Carolina, and near India, Italy, Norway, Denmark, Japan, and Australia.

Russian scientist Alexander Kaffka warns: "There were some important safety rules envisaged at the time; for instance, to dump only in deep waters and far from the shores. But the rules were often broken, which led to the most dangerous kind of dumping — at shallow depths, in straits, and in areas of active fishing."

Mustard gas bombs have washed up on beaches in Poland, Germany, and Australia, and several people in Japan have been killed, with dozens injured, after coming into contact with surfaced nerve agents. Danish fisherman have netted weapons hundreds of times. Some of the ordnance was known to have been leaking before it was sent to the ocean floor, and no one doubts that corrosion has allowed more of the material to escape its containers. The *New York Times* reports: "Scientists from the Baltic countries and Russia have found lethal material mixed in with sediments, and highly toxic sulfur mustard gas, transformed into brown-yellow clumps of gel, has washed ashore."

Still, there's vast disagreement over how much of a threat this material presents. Obviously, most governments think everything's A-OK. The US hasn't even sent a probe to look at the condition of dumped chem-weapons since 1974, and it has no plans to check them ever again. Scientists tend to be more concerned, but some of them caution that doing anything with such huge amounts of poison is riskier than just leaving it alone. ♉

91
CIGARETTE BUTTS ARE THE MOST COMMON TYPE OF LITTER

I don't think I'm alone in becoming so inured to seeing cigarette butts on the ground that I no longer notice them. To our jaded eyes, they blend seamlessly into the landscape, an expected part of the surroundings.

And no wonder. In Westernized countries, they're the most common form of litter; every other piece of trash chucked in public places is the filtered end of a cigarette. The journal *Tobacco Control* estimates that each year over 4.5 *trillion* end up as litter (over 250 billion in the US alone). Add cigarette packs and their cellophane wrappers to the stew, and the situation becomes even worse.

Big Tobacco is eager to foster the belief that their butts are biodegradable, but no study has shown that it takes less than a year for a butt to break down. In fact, some argue that they never truly disintegrate because the filter component is made of cellulose acetate, a form of plastic which never completely goes away.

Besides being an eyesore, the butts are an environmental hazard. Most will eventually get swept into the water supply, where the hundreds of chemicals they contain will be leached out. Fish, seabirds, and other marine creatures have been known to gobble them up, mistaking them for food. If they don't outright poison the critter, they block its digestive and excretory systems. Then there are the kids who nosh on them. It's a relatively small number of children, to be sure, but those illnesses and deaths are preventable. As are the fires caused by flung butts.

Preventing cig litter isn't high up on the tobacco industry's list of priorities, though. They refuse to take many easy steps to help. For one thing, they could put "don't litter" messages on their packages, both in words and with pictograms (a person tossing trash into a wastebasket). Come to think of it, there's nothing stopping them from stamping a message like that on each and every cancer stick they make. Phillip Morris USA has recently said that it puts such messages on "select" packs, which begs the question — why not on *all* packs?

Another action not taken by the industry is to aggressively distribute "personal ashtrays," small, pocket-size receptacles for holding cigarette butts. For a while, RJ Reynolds would send a free pack of thin, foil-lined personal ashtrays to anyone who requested it, but for reasons never explained, they suddenly stopped. The website CigaretteLitter.org writes: "It has long been clear that RJR had no interest in this program being successful as they never promoted it and always made sure they ran out of ashtrays on a frequent basis."

Indeed, if the industry were serious, it could enclose one of these wafer-thin ashtrays in every pack of coffin nails. Or it could sell little plastic devices, about the size of a cigarette lighter, to serve the same purpose, if only they'd design and market them with the same zeal as the cigs themselves. Like the lighter itself, these little disposal units could become an ubiquitous part of the smoker's paraphernalia. Lighters could even have these little ashtrays built in.

Why won't the smoking industry take these and other solid steps? The answers are revealed in internal documents. A Philip Morris memo from March '98 addresses the issue, stating the company's "business objective":

Minimize emergence of regulations resulting in product bans or *committing the Company to take financial and logistical mandated responsibility for disposal of its products and/or packaging.*

An internal report from the Tobacco Institute, the leading industry group, two decades prior says: "Our best course of action may be maintaining a low profile while working to exempt cigarettes from coverage of pending litter control legislation." It recommends that "the concept of courtesy should be limited to the smoking of — rather than the disposal of — tobacco products." The plan notes that "'no-litter' campaigns might be useful; but they should not be implemented before cost/benefit and political analysis has been completed." Researcher Anne Landman of the American Lung Association explains: "[The] document shows that the industry believed that by backing any fees or taxes to help clean up cigarette litter, they would be buying into the 'social cost' argument against smoking."

Of course, when push comes to flick, it's the smoker who tosses the butt on the ground. Those who don't want to contribute to the problem can use public ashtrays or buy pocket versions, such as the pen-shaped, brass "Smart Ashtray" or the colorful, plastic "BUTTsOUT." ☐

92
CAVIAR INVOLVES EXTRAORDINARY CRUELTY

It's no secret that meat comes to us through a process of savage cruelty. For those who care to look, the atrocities inflicted on cows, pigs, chickens, turkeys, and other such creatures are well documented. But one product that often escapes notice is caviar.

True, people consume a lot more hamburgers than fish eggs, but caviar can be found in the refrigerated section of many grocery stores, not to mention every one of the gourmet and "world food" stores that dot most cities. Like fast food joints, though, they're not anxious for us to know how their product got to their shelves.

If you thought that sturgeon nicely laid their eggs somewhere for divers to harmlessly scoop up, forget it. Instead, imagine grabbing a pregnant woman off the street, pimpslapping her, slicing her belly open, ripping out her fetus, then leaving her to slowly die of her injuries and blood loss. That's the human analogy to caviar.

In his investigation of the seedy, greedy worldwide caviar industry, Simon Cooper gives an eyewitness account of a poacher in the Caspian Sea harvesting eggs from the "thick, writhing carpet" of sturgeon he's caught:

The poacher selects a fat female. She is about four feet long and swollen with eggs. He hits her hard with a plank of wood — not hard enough to kill, but enough to stun. Blood trickles from her eyeballs, mouth, and gills. Quickly, the poacher rolls her over, slits open her belly, reaches inside, and carefully extracts a plump, gray-black sac about the size of a pillow. He puts the egg sac into a large plastic bucket and throws the eviscerated fish on the ground, where she flaps and thrashes, her abdomen gaping, until she succumbs and dies. ▢

93
THE HIPPOCRATIC OATH HAS BEEN CHANGED DRAMATICALLY

In almost every medical school when the would-be docs graduate, they recite the Hippocratic oath, pledging to help the sick and behave ethically. This solemn vow, in use since ancient Greek times, is named after the physician Hippocrates, father of Western medicine, although it probably wasn't written by him.

But a Hippocratic oath taken today is not the original oath. While some of the broad ideals are the same, several of the original requirements have been dropped. Originally, the Hippocratic oath was sworn before several gods. You'll occasionally find a contemporary version that invokes one god, but most of them do away with all references to supernatural beings.

Most controversially (to us moderns, anyway), the true oath forbids doctors from performing euthanasia and abortions:

I will neither give a deadly drug to anybody who asked for it, nor will I make a suggestion to this effect. Similarly I will not give to a woman an abortive remedy.

Another section puts the kibosh on hooking up with patients (and, it seems to imply, with patients' family and friends):

Whatever houses I may visit, I will come for the benefit of the sick, remaining free of all intentional injustice, of all mischief and in particular of sexual relations with both female and male persons, be they free or slaves.

Reflecting the Greek system of a mentor imparting medical knowledge to his pupil, the original oath also binds physicians to their teachers for life. If the teacher is ever strapped for cash, his protégé must fork it over. If the teacher has sons, the pupil must regard them as brothers and give them a medical education for free.

Almost all modern versions, including the AMA-approved rendition, do away with these inconvenient precepts. The documentary program *NOVA* reports:

According to a 1993 survey of 150 US and Canadian medical schools, for example, only 14 percent of modern oaths prohibit euthanasia, 11 percent hold covenant with a deity, 8 percent foreswear abortion, and a mere 3 percent forbid sexual contact with patients — all maxims held sacred in the classical version. ♡

94
MOST HYSTERECTOMIES ARE UNNECESSARY

In a hysterectomy, a doctor carves out the uterus and usually the cervix (40 percent of the time, the ovaries are also taken) to deal with a number of conditions ranging from cancer to fibroids to severe PMS. The second-most popular surgical procedure on women, hysterectomies are performed 600,000 times per year in the US. Stanley West, MD, calculates: "At that rate, one out of every three women in this country will have had a hysterectomy by the time she reaches her sixtieth birthday."

The problem is, 70 to 90 percent of the time, the surgery is unnecessary.

For a study published in the journal *Obstetrics and Gynecology*, researchers eyed the cases of 497 women who had undergone the operation. They assembled a panel of physicians who are experts in various specialties to judge whether the procedure was appropriate in each case. The results were dismal: 70 percent of the hysterectomies shouldn't have been done.

Then the researchers judged the operations based on the guidelines set down by the American College of Obstetricians and Gynecologists, and the outcome was even worse: 76 percent of the operations were deemed "inappropriate." The researchers write: "The most common reasons recommendations for hysterectomies [were] considered inappropriate were lack of adequate diagnostic evaluation and failure to try alternative treatments before hysterectomy."

Dr. West, a division chief at St. Vincent's Hospital in New York, goes even further, stating that 90 percent are unnecessary. The operation must be done in cases of uterine cancer, which account for 10 percent of hysterectomies. But, the doc says, every other hysterectomy-inducing disorder can be treated with other, less drastic techniques that avoid or greatly lessen the repercussions of uterus removal — namely, sterility (always), depression, memory loss, and other psychological problems (often), lack of sex drive and response (often), heart disease (increased risk), and death (twelve out of 10,000 women die from the procedure).

Uterine fibroids — the cause of a third of hysterectomies — can be cut out individually, if they truly need to be removed at all. Endometriosis, cysts, pain, abnormal bleeding, PMS, uterine prolapse (in which the uterus loses support and heads south), and pelvic inflammatory disease can be treated by surgeries other than hysterectomies, drugs, alternative therapies, and/or other methods.

Dr. West laments:

The surprisingly outdated attitudes doctors harbor toward female patients are a big part of the problem. Some very old-fashioned views remain embedded in medical training. It may take a few more decades and more medical consumerism on the part of women before the old attitudes give way to a more rational and scientific basis for hysterectomy. ○

95
USING SUNSCREEN CAN CAUSE CANCER

It's easy to think that slathering on sunscreen will make you practically invulnerable to skin cancer. Those evil rays will just bounce off you *à la* Superman. The manufacturers of these products don't exactly go out of their way to let you know
that this isn't the case.

Most sunscreens only block the ultraviolet rays known as UVB, which cause sunburn and, in the long term, some skin cancer. But they do very little, next to nothing, to filter out the longer UVA rays, which also trigger skin cancer (in fact, UVA is probably more likely to do so). In other words, while you are prevented from being fried like a lobster, other rays that cause serious long-term health problems are pounding your skin unabated.

Often, wearing sunscreen only makes things worse, because people tend to stay outside

longer when they think they're protected by coconut-scented body armor. Thus, they drink up more of the killer UVA.

And let's not forget that it's absolutely crucial for us to get Vitamin D, which is formed when our bods are exposed UVB, the very wavelength being stopped in its tracks by sunscreen. Among other things, D protects against some cancers, including breast and colon.

To drive another nail into sunscreen's coffin, be aware that when you use it, you're smearing loads of chemicals, some toxic, onto your skin, which drinks them up like soda and pipes them right into your body.

So what's a Sun worshipper to do? Ditch the lotions altogether. Spend small amounts of time in the Sun until your skin acclimates and you're able to stay exposed longer — an hour a day — without turning red. If you have to be outside longer, use clothing and things like beach umbrellas to keep the excess rays off your skin. Dr. Joseph Mercola boils it down: "The key is to never burn." ⌀

96
INVOLUNTARY HUMAN EXPERIMENTATION IS NOT A THING OF THE PAST

A study conducted by Johns Hopkins University, published in the *Journal of Medical Ethics*, asked hundreds of "health researchers in developing countries" if their studies using human subjects were being screened by ethics boards. The findings were bleak: 44 percent of respondents said that no one reviews their use of human guinea pigs. Of these unchecked experiments, US corporations and nonprofits fund one-third. Regarding the studies that were reviewed, in 92 percent of the cases, the ethics board of the institution performing the experiment did the screening, with no input from higher-level bodies. The study unearthed another fundamental problem — cases in which the patient consent forms weren't in the host country's language.

Not that all researchers even bother with consent forms. In the past few years, India has been roiled by revelations of several illegal drug trials that resulted in deaths. Some of the country's largest biotech and drug-manufacturing companies are neck-deep in scandals involving elderly people, sterile women, and cancer patients all being given experimental drugs without their knowledge. (In the cancer case, the secret trials were performed for a researcher at Johns Hopkins).

But undeveloped countries are hardly the only sites of Mengelean medical ethics. Pediatric drug testing on orphans in the US has almost completely escaped public scrutiny, but independent investigative reporter Liam Scheff is lifting the lid. (Due to their utter powerlessness, orphans have always been favored lab rats for medical experimentation.) ICC — a Catholic charity under the auspices of the Archdiocese of New York — houses children who tested HIV-positive or who were born to mothers with HIV. These kids have been guinea pigs for dozens of drug experiments funded by government agencies and pharmaceutical companies. They're given extremely toxic drugs, such as AZT, sometimes while they're still in the crib.

While some involved parties claim that the kids are simply being given wonderful cutting-edge drugs, documents obtained by the London *Observer* show that some trials have tested the "safety and tolerance" and "toxicity" of HIV drugs and the "tolerance [and] safety" of herpes drugs. The *Observer* reports that an "experiment sponsored by Glaxo and US drug firm Pfizer investigated the 'long-term safety' of anti-bacterial drugs on three-month-old babies." One study is titled, "The Safety and Effectiveness of Treating Advanced AIDS Patients between the Ages 4 and 22 with Seven Drugs, Some at Higher than Usual Doses." Children who refuse to take the drugs have a hole surgically drilled into their abdomen, so that the meds can be shunted directly into their bodies. ⌂

97
HEAD TRANSPLANTS ON MONKEYS HAVE ALREADY BEEN PERFORMED

The successful transplant of a primate's head from its own body to that of another must rank as one of the greatest medical achievements of the twentieth century, if not all time. Even if it didn't usher in a brave new world of head/brain/body transplants for humans, it would surely be embedded in the mass mind like Dolly the cloned sheep. But that isn't how it happened.

Dr. Robert White — at the time, a neurosurgeon at Cleveland's Metro Health Care Center — experimented with keeping disembodied monkey and dog brains alive during the 1960s. In 1970, he upped the ante by severing the head of a rhesus monkey, then attaching it to the headless, still-living body of a second monkey. An article from London's *Sunday Telegraph Magazine* sets the scene of the 18-hour surgery:

Chalk marks on the floor fixed the positions of more than thirty highly drilled professionals: two surgical teams, a squad of anaesthesiologists, assorted nurses, phalanxes of technicians, a bevy of scientists equipped to analyse blood and urine samples on the spot.

The poor creature regained consciousness and, according to White's paper in *Surgery*, it and the subsequent Frankenmonkeys were well aware of their surroundings, visually tracking people and objects. Traumatized beyond all comprehension, they were also agitated and violent, chomping a staff member's finger "if orally stimulated." In her death book *Stiff*, Mary Roach writes:

When White placed food in their mouths, they chewed it and attempted to swallow it — a bit of a dirty trick, given that the esophagus hadn't been reconnected and was now a dead end. The monkeys lived anywhere from six hours to three days, most of them dying from rejection issues or from bleeding.

Although this amazing and troubling procedure initially generated headlines, it's been largely forgotten. In the past few years, isolated articles on White's work have popped up in the British mainstream media and the American alternative press (*Wired* and the *Cleveland Scene*, for example). But this seemingly impossible feat failed to become common knowledge.

White caught a lot of heat from bioethicists, fellow doctors, and animal rights activists. This, plus the expense of these operations, meant that he had to give up this field of research. Still, during his occasional interviews, he dreams of pulling the ol' switcheroo on human noggins. Several countries less prone to hand-wringing have expressed interest, he says, but the funding just isn't there. And who wants to be the first head on the chopping block? The procedure would be of most benefit to paralyzed people whose bodies are in danger of giving out. Because medical science still can't reconnect severed spinal nerves, any recipient would be unable to move below the neck. Once the people in white coats overcome this limitation, White could find himself back in business. And heads will roll. ⌖

Dr. White isn't the only scientist who's been playing musical heads. Optometrist and anatomist Paul Pietsch has fricasseed salamanders — their brains, heads, and eyes — in every conceivable combination. Not as impressive as higher primates, but the results have been at least as good. Pietsch has successfully attached an embryonic head to the eye socket of a young salamander. The second head became sentient, but the host croaked after a few months.

Another poor amphibian, charmingly nicknamed Brainless, had its entire brain (except for the medulla oblongata) carved out of its head. He survived by being force-fed but naturally was never again active.

Then there was Punky, the salamander who was given the brain of a frog. As theorized, the little guy quit snarfing up tiny worms — a salamander delicacy — and instead lived peaceably with them, as frogs do.

98
SCIENTISTS ARE RECREATING THE 1918 SPANISH FLU VIRUS

The year from spring 1918 to spring 1919 saw one of the worst epidemics — perhaps even *the* worst — in human history. The Spanish flu raced around the globe, killing 20 to 50 million people. That's a higher body count than World War I. More than the "Black Death" in medieval Europe. The Human Virology website at Stanford University explains:

An estimated 675,000 Americans died of influenza during the pandemic, ten times as many as in the world war. Of the US soldiers who died in Europe, half of them fell to the influenza virus and not to the enemy. ...

The effect of the influenza epidemic was so severe that the average life span in the US was depressed by 10 years. The influenza virus had a profound virulence, with a mortality rate at 2.5% compared to the previous influenza epidemics, which were less than 0.1%.

The *Encyclopedia Britannica* avers: "Outbreaks of the flu occurred in nearly every inhabited part of the world..." Some people died less than 24 hours after catching the bug. Oddly, it was most likely to cut down young adults, rather than the usual targets of influenza — children and the elderly.

You get the idea — it was a worldwide catastrophe that could've easily caused societies to crumble. Thank goodness it could never happen again. Well, that's actually not a sure thing. Not content to leave well enough alone, scientists are in the process of *recreating* the Spanish flu virus.

Dr. Jeffrey Taubenberger from the US Armed Forces Institute of Pathology found portions of the killer in tissue samples from the time period. He and his colleagues were able to decode several genetic sequences, which they published.

Taking it to the next level, they teamed up with other scientists to partially resurrect the virus. In 2001, they spliced a gene from the 1918 flu into a run-of-the-mill flu virus. The next year, they did the same trick, only this time they added two 1918 genes into the mix. The resulting patchwork virus killed mice at a much higher level than current strains. The Sunshine Project, a watchdog organization fighting the development of biological weapons, warns: "This experiment is only one step away from taking the 1918 demon entirely out of the bottle and bringing the Spanish flu back to life."

Why take such a huge risk by reanimating a defunct killer of millions of people? The scientists have varying explanations. To study influenza in general. To figure out what made this virus so deadly and if it could happen again. To develop a vaccine against the 1918 virus (which no one would need if the virus weren't brought back in the first place). Simply because the scientists wanted to test out some new techniques, and, as Taubenberger told the American Society for Microbiology: "The 1918 flu was by far and away the most interesting thing we could think of…" Yet another reason was to keep the Institute's massive collection of 60 million tissue samples from being tossed out as a cost-cutting measure. Taubenberger: "Everyone was bending over backwards to see what part of the government they could cut away next, so I want to make my own little contribution and point out why it would be prudent to keep this place in business."

While those first two goals are worthwhile in theory, we might sleep more soundly if they were approached in different ways. Couldn't scientists just examine the genetic code without actually cooking up the virus? Won't computer simulations work? If you trust that harmful viruses don't escape from labs, you haven't read the Department of Agriculture Inspector General's report on lax conditions at facilities housing these nasty beasts. This 2003 tongue-lashing said:

Security measures at 20 of the 104 laboratories were not commensurate with the risk associated with the pathogens they housed. These 20 laboratories represented over half of the laboratories in our sample that stored high con-

sequence pathogens. Alarm systems, surveillance cameras, and identification badges were commonly lacking in buildings housing the laboratories, and key-card devices or sign-in sheets were not generally used to record entries to the laboratories.

It gave this reassuring example:

We discovered a Centers for Disease Control and Prevention (CDC) select agent at one institution that was kept in an unsecured freezer and for which no risk assessment had been made. The agent, Yersinia pestis, causes bubonic and pneumonic plague and requires strict containment. The freezer that stored this agent had not been inventoried since 1994, when a box of unidentified pathogens was already noted as missing.

Hmm, I'm feeling a little feverish....

99
THE VATICAN, INCLUDING THE POPE, IS DIRECTLY INVOLVED IN THE CATHOLIC CHURCH'S PEDOPHILE COVER-UP

It took several decades, but in 2002 the media finally gave due attention to the epidemic of priests who molest children and the higher-ups who transfer the perps to other dioceses, where they choose from a fresh crop of potential victims. The press was rightly unsparing when it came to naming priests, bishops, archbishops, and cardinals in the US, but that courage didn't extend past America's borders. Except in exceedingly rare instances, the media couldn't work up the nerve to point fingers at the Vatican. Despite this conspicuous blind spot, several unearthed documents directly implicate the highest levels of the Catholic Church, including three Popes, in the cover-up.

The earliest such document — "Instruction on the Manner of Proceeding in Cases of Solicitation" — was sent to every high-ranking cleric in the world in 1962 (it was uncovered during legal action in 2003). It explains what to do when a priest gets accused of sexual acts with a penitent (someone whose confession they'd heard), a child, or an animal. The gist is that the offending man of the cloth is to be secretly tried by local Church officials (or, in some cases, the Vatican's Holy Office). Secular authorities are not to be alerted, and all paperwork is to be walled up in the diocese's "secret archive."

The "Instruction" includes a secrecy clause regarding these transgressions — an oath to be recited in which the cleric swears "under the pain of excommunication" and "other most serious penalties" that he will "observe this secret absolutely and in every way," never "directly or indirectly" revealing anything, "even for the most urgent and most serious cause [even] for the purpose of a greater good."

A note at the end of the main body declares that the "Instruction" was issued by "the most eminent Cardinal Secretary of the Holy Office" and was personally approved by Pope John XXIII.

Priest James Porter pled guilty to molesting 28 children during the 1960s and early 1970s (the actual count is believed to be around 100 kids in five states). Documents show that his superiors, fully aware of his serial child-rape, shuffled him to one diocese after another. In 2002, a *Boston Herald* lawsuit forced the release of Porter's file. It turns out that the pedo-priest had written a letter directly to Pope Paul VI in 1973, confessing his molestations and asking the Pontiff to let him out of the priesthood. It's not known how the Pope responded, but the next year Porter was no longer a priest. It wasn't until 20 years later that many of his victims banded together and got him sent to prison. Although they undoubtedly were aware of earlier cases, this provides documentary proof that the highest levels of the Vatican knew what was happening by 1973, at the latest.

The most recent smoking document proving the Pope's awareness and complicity dates back just a few years. (It too was publicly released during the scandal of 2002.) Dated May 29, 1999, the order signed by Pope John Paul calls for the defrocking of Robert Burns, a priest who pled guilty to indecent assault of a child. In it, his Holiness says that the molester "ought to live away from the places where his previous condition is known." However, wrote the Pope, the diocese doesn't have to ship him elsewhere "if it is foreseen that the presence of the suppliant will cause no scandal."

Lawyer Roderick MacLeish, who handles sex abuse lawsuits against the Church, told Reuters:

"For the first time we've seen documents from the Vatican that emphasize the word that we've seen so often here in Boston — 'scandal.' This document says he is to be relocated to another place where presumably they wouldn't know about him, unless the bishop or the cardinal of the appropriate diocese determines it will cause no scandal. What about the children?" ⌑

100
GOD'S NAME IS "JEALOUS"

There's an old joke that says God's name is Harold, as in: "Our Father, who art in Heaven, Harold be thy name…"

The strange thing is, that's not too much off the mark, only the truth is even weirder. The LORD does indeed have a name, kind of like Andrew or Beth or José.

It's right there in the Bible, at Exodus 34:13. Moses has trudged up Mount Sinai with a second pair of stone tablets, on which God will write the Ten Commandments. Moses and the Big G engage in some repartee, then God says:

"For thou shalt worship no other god: for the LORD, whose name is Jealous, is a jealous God"

This is straight out of the King James Version. God reveals "his" own name: Jealous.

In the original Hebrew, the key words in this verse are *shem* and *qanna'*. According to one of the standard reference works in this area — *A Concise Dictionary of the Words in the Hebrew Bible* by James Strongs — *shem* is a noun meaning "name." One of its specific denotations is "the Name (as designation of God)." The word *qanna'* means "jealous" and is applied only to God.

Other English translations say the same basic thing as the King James Version. The New International Version gives it as: "Do not worship any other god, for the LORD, whose name is Jealous, is a jealous God." The English Standard Version phrases it parenthetically: "(for you shall worship no other god, for the LORD, whose name is Jealous, is a jealous God)." The New International Readers Version gives God a more relaxed feel: "Do not worship any other god. I am a jealous God. In fact, my name is Jealous."

Why isn't this mentioned in Sunday school? Perhaps because it could lead to children pledging, "One nation, under Jealous," people cursing, "Jealous damn it!" or the government stamping on currency: "In Jealous we trust."

But if you're going to accept the Bible, then you have to accept it when God reveals his own name, no matter how odd or silly.

May Jealous have mercy on my soul. ▯

REFERENCES

Ten Commandments. Book of Exodus, King James Bible.

Pope's Erotic Book. Piccolomini, Aeneas Silvius (Pius II). *The Goodli History of the Ladye Lucres of Scene and of Her Lover Eurialus.* Edited by E.J. Morrall. Oxford University Press, 1996. • Website of James O'Donnell, former professor of classical studies at the University of Pennsylvania [ccat.sas.upenn.edu/jod/]. • Translations from early English into modern English by Russ Kick.

CIA Crimes. Kelly, John. "Crimes and Silence." *Into the Buzzsaw: Leading Journalists Expose the Myth of a Free Press.* Edited by Kristina Borjesson. Amherst, NY: Prometheus Books, 2002, pp 311-31. • Permanent Select Committee on Intelligence, US House of Representatives, 104th Congress. "IC21: The Intelligence Community in the 21st Century." Government Printing Office, 1996, chapter 9: "Clandestine Service."

CIA Agent. Gup, Ted. *The Book of Honor: Covert Lives and Classified Deaths at the CIA.* Doubleday (Random House), 2000. • Further reading: Laird, Thomas. *Into Tibet: The CIA's First Atomic Spy and His Secret Expedition to Lhasa.* Grove Press, 2002.

Afghanistan's Food Supply. Woodward, Bob, and Dan Balz. "Combating Terrorism: 'It Starts Today.'" ("10 Days in September," part 6). *Washington Post,* 1 Feb 2002. • This revelation was first unburied by Matthew Rothschild, editor of *The Progressive.*

Terrorism Convictions. Fazlollah, Mark. "Reports of Terror Crimes Inflated." *Philadelphia Inquirer,* 15 May 2003. • Fazlollah, Mark, and Peter Nicholas. "US Overstates Arrests in Terrorism." *Philadelphia Inquirer,* 16 Dec 2001. • United States General Accounting Office. "Justice Department: Better Management Oversight and Internal Controls Needed to Ensure Accuracy of Terrorism-Related Statistics." Jan 2003.

Provoking Terrorist Attack. Arkin, William M. "The Secret War." *Los Angeles Times,* 27 Oct 2002. • Defense Science Board. "DBS Summer Study on Special Operations and Joint Forces in Support of Counter Terrorism, Final Outbrief," 16 Aug 2002 (declassified version). • Floyd, Chris. "Global Eye -- Into the Dark." *Moscow Times,* 1 Nov 2002. • Hess, Pamela. "Panel Wants $7bn Elite Counter-terror Unit." United Press International, 26 Sept 2002.

Nuking the Moon. Barnett, Antony. "US Planned One Big Nuclear Blast for Mankind." *Observer* (London), 14 May 2000. • Davidson, Keay. *Carl Sagan: A Life.* New York: John Wiley & Sons, 1999. • Ulivi, Paolo. "Nuke the Moon!" Grand Tour Planetary Exploration Page [utenti.lycos.it/paoloulivi/], 13 Oct 2002. Ulivi is an engineer and the author of an upcoming book on unmanned lunar exploration from Springer-Praxis Publishing Ltd. • Zabarenko, Deborah. "Moon Bomb?" Reuters News Agency, 17 May 2000. • Zheleznyakov, Aleksandr. "The E-4 Project: Exploding a Nuclear Bomb on the Moon."

Enciklopediya Kosmonavtika [*Cosmonautics Encyclopedia*]. Translated by Sven Grahn of the Swedish Space Corporation [www.svengrahn.pp.se/ histind/E3/E3orig.htm].

Nuking North Carolina. The Goldsboro incident remained shrouded in mystery and misinformation until four students at the University of North Carolina at Chapel Hill did loads of original research (interviews, FOIA requests, etc.) and created a Website called Broken Arrow: Goldsboro, NC <www.ibiblio.org/bomb/>. It is by far the definitive source of information on this almost-catastrophe. The students are Cliff Nelson, Nick Harrison, Andrew Leung, and Megan E. Butler.

World War III. Kozlov, Yuriy, and Aleksandr Stepanenko. "Norwegian Rocket Incident Settled." ITAR-TASS (Moscow), 27 Jan 1995. • Krieger, David. "Crisis and Opportunity." Website of the Nuclear Age Peace Foundation [www.wagingpeace.org], 2002. • The Back From the Brink Campaign. *Short Fuse to Catastrophe: The Case for Taking Nuclear Weapons Off Hair-trigger Alert* (briefing book). Self-published, 2001, p 4. [www.backfromthebrink.org].

Korean War Never Ended. Hermes, Walter. "Armistice Negotiations." *The Korean War: An Encyclopedia.* Ed. by Stanley Sandler. Garland Publishing, 1995. • Levie, Howard S. "Armistice." *Crimes of War: What the Public Should Know.* Ed. by Roy Gutman and David Rieff. W.W. Norton & Co., 1999. • Text of the Korean War Armistice Agreement, 27 July 1953. • Unsigned. "The Korean War Armistice." BBC News, 18 Feb 2003.

Agent Orange in Korea. "Agent Orange and Related Issues." Department of Veterans Affairs Fact Sheet, Jan 2003. • "Agent Orange Outside of Viet Nam." *News and Notes for Florida Veterans*, Apr 2003. Department of Veterans Affairs, St. Petersburg Regional Office. • Jelinek, Pauline. "Some to Get Agent Orange Testing." Associated Press, 3 Nov 2000. • VHA Directive 2000-027: Registry Examinations for Veterans Possibly Exposed to Agent Orange in Korea. Department of Veterans Affairs, Veterans Health Administration, 5 Sept 2000.

Student Massacres. Cabell, Brian, and Matt Smith. "S.C. College Marks 'Orangeburg Massacre' Anniversary." CNN, 8 Feb 2001. • Sellers, Cleveland. "The Orangeburg Massacre, 1968." *It Did Happen Here: Recollections of Political Repression in America.* Ed. by Bud Schultz and Ruth Schultz. University of California Press, 1989. • Spofford, Tim. *Lynch Street: The May 1970 Slayings at Jackson State College.* Kent State University Press, 1988. • "The May 1970 Tragedy at Jackson State University." Jackson State University Website. [http://www.jsums.edu/~www/gg02.htm]. • Further reading: Nelson, Jack, and Jack Bass. *The Orangeburg Massacre* (second edition). Mercer University Press, 1999.

Churchill. Churchill, Winston. "Zionism Versus Bolshevism: A Struggle for the Soul of the Jewish People." *Illustrated Sunday Herald* (London), 8 Feb 1920. An image of the original article as it was printed has been widely reproduced on the Web. • "Sir Winston Churchill." Biography on the BBC Website. • Woods, Frederick. *A Bibliography of the Works of Sir Winston Churchill, KG, OM, CH, MP.* University of Toronto Press, 1963: p 186.

REFERENCES

Auschwitz Tattoo. Black, Edwin. "The IBM Link to Auschwitz." *Village Voice*, 9 Oct 2002.

Hitler's Relatives. Gardner, David. *The Last of the Hitlers*. BMM, 2001. Gardner doesn't reveal the Hitlers' new last name nor the town in which they live.

Male Witches. Apps, Lara, and Andrew Gow. *Male Witches in Early Modern Europe*. Manchester University Press, 2003.

Cannibal Colonists. Zinn, Howard. *A People's History of the United States* (Perennial Classics Edition). HarperCollins Publishers, 2001, p 24. (Originally published 1980.)

Feminists Against Abortion. Taken directly from the writings of Anthony, Stanton, Blackwell, and Woodhull and Claflin, reproduced in MacNair, Rachel, Mare Krane Derr, and Linda Naranjo-Huebl (eds.). *Prolife Feminism: Yesterday and Today*. Sulzburger & Graham Publishing, 1995.

Black Confederates. Barrow, Charles Kelly, J.H. Segars, and R.B. Rosenburg. *Black Confederates*. Pelican Publishing Company, 2001. • Segars, J.H., and Charles Kelly Barrow. *Black Southerners in Confederate Armies: A Collection of Historical Accounts*. Southern Lion Books, 2001.

Electric Cars. Didik, Frank. "History and Directory of Electric Cars from 1834–1987." Didik Design Website [www.didik.com], 2001. • Rae, John B. "The Electric Vehicle Company: A Monopoly that Missed." *Business History Review*, 1955. • Schallenberg, Richard H. "Prospects for the Electric Vehicle: A Historical Perspective." *IEEE Transactions on Education*, vol. E-23, No 3, Aug 1980. • Schiffer, Michael Brian, with Tamara C. Butts and Kimberly K. Grimm. *Taking Charge: The Electric Automobile in America*. Smithsonian Institution Press, 1994. • Wakefield, Ernest Henry, PhD. *History of the Electric Automobile: Hybrid Electric Vehicles*. Society of Automotive Engineers, 1998.

Juries. Conrad, Clay S. *Jury Nullification: The Evolution of a Doctrine*. Carolina Academic Press, 1998. • Various literature from the Fully Informed Jury Association, [www.fija.org], 1-800-TEL-JURY, PO Box 5570, Helena MT 59604.

Police Nonprotection. Stevens, Richard W. *Dial 911 and Die: The Shocking Truth About the Police Protection Myth*. Mazel Freedom Press, 1999.

Government Can Take Your Home. Berliner, Dana. *Government Theft: Top 10 Abuses of Eminent Domain, 1998-2002*. Castle Coalition (a project of the Institute for Justice), 2003. • Berliner, Dana. *Public Power, Private Gain: A Five-Year, State-by-State Report Examining the Abuse of Eminent Domain*. Castle Coalition (a project of the Institute for Justice), Apr 2003.

Supreme Court on Drugs. Gray, Judge James P. *Why Our Drug Laws Have Failed and What We Can Do About It: A Judicial*

Indictment of the War on Drugs. Temple University Press, 2001. • *Linder v. United States*, 925. No. 183. U.S. Supreme Court 268 U.S. 5 (1925). • *Robinson v. California*. SCT.1193, 370 U.S. 660, 82 S. Ct. 1417, 8 L. Ed. 2d 758 (1962). • *Powell v. Texas*, 392 U.S. 514 (1968) (USSC).

Age of Consent. For the US, actual text of state laws. The Age of Consent Website [www.ageofconsent.com] contains all the relevant state codes, as well as links to the code on official state Websites. The site also has primarily official documentation (often from Interpol) regarding the laws in other countries.

Scientists' Citations. Muir, Hazel. "Scientists Exposed as Sloppy Reporters." *New Scientist*, 14 Dec 2002.

Pasteur. Waller, John. *Einstein's Luck: The Truth Behind Some of the Greatest Scientific Discoveries*. Oxford University Press, 2002: Chapter 1, "The Pasteurization of Spontaneous Generation," pp 14-31. (Published in the UK as *Fabulous Science*.)

GAIA Nuclear Power. Lovelock, James. Preface to *Environmentalists for Nuclear Energy* by Bruno Comby. TNR Editions, 1995.

Genetically-Engineered Humans. Barritt, Jason A., *et al*. "Mitochondria in Human Offspring Derived From Ooplasmic Trans-plantation." *Human Reproduction*, 16.3 (2001), pp 513-6. • Email communication from Dr. Joseph Cummins, 4 June 2003. • "First Cases of Human Germline Genetic Modification Announced." *British Medical Journal* 322 (12 May 2001), p 1144. • "Genetically Modified Human Babies?" Australian Broadcasting Corporation, 8 May 2001. • Hawes, S.M., C. Sapienza, and K.E. Latham. "Ooplasmic Donation in Humans: The Potential for Epigenic Modifications." *Human Reproduction* 17.4 (2002), 850-2. • Hill, Amelia. "Horror at 'Three Parent Foetus' Gene Disorders." *Observer* (London), 20 May 2001. • Turner Syndrome Society Website [www.turner-syndrome-us.org].

Insurance Industry. Black, Edwin. *War Against the Weak: Eugenics and America's Campaign to Create a Master Race*. Four Walls Eight Windows, 2003, pp 432-5.

Smoking. The American Council on Science and Health. *Cigarettes: What the Warning Label Doesn't Tell You*. Prometheus Books, 1997.

Bovine Leukemia. Buehring, G.C., K.Y. Choi, and H.M. Jensen. "Bovine Leukemia Virus in Human Breast Tissues." *Breast Cancer Research* 2001 3(Suppl 1):A14. • Buehring, Gertrude, PhD. "Bovine Leukemia Virus Infection and Human Breast Cancer Risk." Grant proposal and final report, 2002. • Kradjian, Robert M., MD. "The Milk Letter: A Message to My Patients." Website of American Fitness Professionals and Associates [www.afpafitness.com], no date. Kradjian is chief of breast surgery, Division of General Surgery, Seton Medical Centre, Daly City, CA. • USDA. "High Prevalence of BLV in US Dairy Herds." Info sheet from the Animal and Plant Health Inspection Service, US Department of Agriculture, undated.

CAT Scans. Wysong, Pippa. "Doctors Have Little More Info Than Patients About CT Scan Safety." *Medical Post* 39.20 (20 May 2003). • "Computed Tomography Imaging (CT Scan, CAT Scan)" on Imaginis.com.

Medication Errors. Regush, Nicholas. "Medication Errors: Too Little Attention." RedFlagsDaily e-newsletter, 30 May 2003. • Ricks, Delthia. "Poison in Prescription: Illegible Writing Can Lead to Dangerous Medication Errors." *Newsday* (New York), 19 Mar 2001. • Waters, Rob. "Precarious Prescriptions: Can Your Doctor's Handwriting Kill You?" WebMD, 4 Aug 2000. • Website of the United States Pharmacopeial Convention, Inc. [www.usp.org].

Prescription Drugs. Graham, Garthe K., Sidney M. Wolfe, *et al.* "Postmarketing Surveillance and Black Box Warnings." JAMA 288 (2002), pp 955-9. • Lazarou, Jason, M.Sc., Bruce H. Pomeranz, MD, PhD, and Paul N. Corey, PhD. "Incidence of Adverse Drug Reactions in Hospitalized Patients: A Meta-analysis of Prospective Studies." JAMA 279 (1998), pp 1200-5. • Website of the Food and Drug Administration [www.fda.gov]. • Wolfe, Sidney, MD. "Statement by Sidney Wolfe: Recent Events Arguing Against Things Getting Better as Suggested by the FDA Editorial in Tomorrow's JAMA." Public Citizen Website [www.citizen.org], circa 1 May 2002.

Work Kills. International Labor Organization. "Workers' Memorial Day Ceremony to Focus on Emergency Workers, Firefighters." Press release, 24 Apr 2002. • Cullen, Lisa. *A Job to Die For: Why So Many Americans Are Killed, Injured or Made Ill at Work and What to Do About It.* Common Courage Press, 2002. This book uses the following as its sources for the US statistics I've cited: Bureau of Labor Statistics and *Costs of Occupational Injuries and Illnesses* by J. Paul Leigh (University of Michigan Press, 2000).

Elder Suicide. US statistics are for the latest available year (2000) and are from the Centers for Disease Control and Prevention, particularly their Web-based Injury Statistics Query and Reporting System [www.cdc.gov/ncipc/wisqars/] and their factsheet "Suicide in the United States." • Global statistics are from the World Health Organisation's graph: "Distribution of suicide rates (per 100,000), by gender and age, 1998." Located on the WHO's international site [www.who.int].

HIV Tests. Gigerenzer, Gerd. *Calculated Risks: How to Know When Numbers Deceive You.* Simon & Schuster, 2002.

DNA Matching. Gigerenzer, Gerd. *Calculated Risks: How to Know When Numbers Deceive You.* Simon & Schuster, 2002. • Thompson, W.C., F. Taroni, and C.G. Aitken. "How the Probability of a False Positive Affects the Value of DNA Evidence." *Journal of Forensic Sciences* 48.1 (Jan 2003). • Website of L.D. Mueller, professor of biology at the University of California Irvine School of Biological Sciences [darwin.bio.uci.edu/~mueller/]. • Website of *Scientific Testimony*, an online journal devoted to forensic evidence, "edited and published by faculty and students of the Department of Criminology, Law & Society, University of California, Irvine" [www.scientific.org].

Lie Detectors. Opening Statement on Polygraph Screening, by Supervisory Special Agent Dr. Drew C. Richardson, FBI Laboratory Division, before the United States Senate Committee on the Judiciary, Subcommittee on Administrative Oversight and the Courts, Senate Hearing 105-431: A Review of the Federal Bureau of Investigation Laboratory: Beyond the Inspector General Report, 29 Sept 1997. Available at antipolygraph.org.

Bayer. Askwith, Richard. "How Aspirin Turned Hero." *Sunday Times* (London), 13 Sept 1998. • Bogdanich, Walt, and Eric Koli. "2 Paths of Bayer Drug in 80's: Riskier Type Went Overseas." *New York Times*, 22 May 2003. • Metzger, Th. *The Birth of Heroin and the Demonization of the Dope Fiend*. Loompanics Unlimited, 1998.

LSD Therapy. Grof, Stanislav, MD. *LSD Psychotherapy: Exploring the Frontiers of the Hidden Mind*. Hunter House, 1980, 1994. • "Psychedelic Research Around the World" page [www.maps.org/research/] on the Website of the Multidisciplinary Association for Psychedelic Studies. • "LSD: The Drug," Website of the Drug Enforcement Administration [www.usdoj.gov/dea/].

Sagan. Davidson, Keay. *Carl Sagan: A Life*. New York: John Wiley & Sons, 1999. • Grinspoon, Lester. *Marihuana Reconsidered*. Harvard University Press, 1971.

Black Hawk Down. Turner, Megan. "War Film 'Hero' Is a Rapist." *New York Post*, 18 Dec 2001.

SUV Drivers. Bradsher, Keith. *High and Mighty: SUVs—The World's Most Dangerous Vehicles and How They Got That Way*. PublicAffairs (Perseus). 2002. pp 101-7.

"Squaw." Bright, William. "The Sociolinguistics of the 'S-Word': 'Squaw' in American Placenames." Undated article posted to Dr. Bright's Website at the Northern California Indian Development Council [www.ncidc.org/bright/]. • Bruchac, Marge. "Reclaiming the Word 'Squaw' in the Name of the Ancestors." NativeWeb, Nov 1999.

Mailing Letters. Mr. Unzip. *How to Screw the Post Office*. Loompanics Unlimited, 2000.

Advertisers' Influence. Fleetwood, Blake. "The Broken Wall: How Newspapers Are Selling Their Credibility to Advertisers." *Washington Monthly*, Sept 1999. • Kerwin, Ann Marie. "Advertiser Pressure on Newspapers Is Common: Survey." *Editor and Publisher*, 16 Jan 1993. • The Project for Excellence in Journalism. "Local TV News Project – 2002: Investigative Journalism Despite the Odds." On their Website [www.journalism.org].

Art Forgery. Hoving, Thomas. *False Impressions: The Hunt for Big-Time Art Fakes*. Simon & Schuster, 1996. • Nash, Elizabeth. "Was There a Family Conspiracy to Cover up the Truth About Goya's Finest Work?" *Independent* (London), 1 May 2003.

REFERENCES

Male Clits. Blackledge, Catherine. *The Story of V: A Natural History of Female Sexuality*. Rutgers University Press, 2004. § Gray, Henry. *Anatomy of the Human Body*. 20th ed., rev. and re-edited by Warren H. Lewis. Philadelphia: Lea & Febiger, 1918. § Sevely, Josephine Lowndes. *Eve's Secrets: A New Theory of Female Sexuality*. Random House, 1987.

False Dads. American Association of Blood Banks. "Annual Report Summary for Testing in 1999." No date. § American Association of Blood Banks. "Annual Report Summary for Testing in 2001." Oct 2002. § Baker, Robin. Ph.D. *Sperm Wars: The Science of Sex*. HarperCollins, 1996. § Child Support Analysis website. "Misattributed Paternity." 5 July 2004. [www.childsupportanalysis.co.uk]. § Gallagher, Caoilfhionn. "In the Name of the Father? Legal and Ethical Dilemmas Surrounding 'Accidental' Findings of Non-Paternity." Annual Conference 2003, Socio-Legal Studies Association at Nottigham Law School. [www.nls.ntu.ac.uk/slsa2003/]. § Lucassen, Anneke and Michael Parker. "Revealing False Paternity: Some Ethical Considerations" *Lancet* 357 (2001): 1033-5. § Philipp, E. "Discussion: Moral, Social and Ethical Issues." *Law and Ethics of A.I.D. and Embryo Transfer*. Ciba Foundation Symposium (Vol. 17), G.E.W. Wostenholme and D.W. Fitzsimons (eds.). Amsterdam: Elsevier, Excerpta Medica, North-Holland, 1973: 63-66.

Old Porn. *1000 Nudes: Uwe Scheid Collection*. Benedikt Taschen, 1994. § Cooper, Emmanuel. *Fully Exposed: The Male Nude in Photography* (second ed.). Routledge, 1995. § Coopersmith, Jonathan. "Pornography, Technology and Progress." *Icon* 4 (1998). § Nazarieff, Serge. *Early Erotic Photography*. Benedikt Taschen, 1993. § Nazarieff, Serge. *Stereo Akte/Nudes/Nus*. Benedikt Taschen, 1993. § Neret, Gilles. *Erotica Universalis*. Benedikt Taschen, 1994. § Simons, G.L. *The Illustrated Book of Sexual Records*. 1974, 1982, 1997-2001. Online version at [www.world-sex-records.com]. § Website of Barcelonan artist Daniel Verdejo [www.arterupestre-c.com]. § Kinsey Institute website [www.kinseyinstitute.org].

Shakespeare. Macrone, Michael. *Naughty Shakespeare*. Andrews McMeel, 1997. § Partridge, Eric. *Shakespeare's Bawdy* (fourth edition). Routledge, 2001. Originally 1947.

Barbie. Lord, M.G. *Forever Barbie: The Unauthorized Biography of a Real Doll*. William Morrow and Company, 1994. § Doll Reference: Vintage Dolls 1951-1976. [members.tripod.com/ltanis/]. § Dolls and Toys Australia. [www.dollsandtoysaustralia.com].

Fetuses. Blackledge, Catherine. *The Story of V: A Natural History of Female Sexuality*. Rutgers University Press, 2004. § Edell, Dean. *Eat, Drink, and Be Merry: America's Doctor Tells You Why the Health Experts Are Wrong*. HarperCollins, 1999: 209. § Giorgi, G, and M. Siccardi. "Ultrasonographic Observation of a Female Fetus' Sexual Behavior in Utero." *American Journal of Obstetrics and Gynecology* 175 (Sept 1996): 753. § Meizner, I. "Sonographic Observation of in Utero Fetal 'Masturbation'." *Journal of Ultrasound Medicine* 6.2 (Feb 1987): 111. § Taylor, Timothy. *The Prehistory of Sex: Four Million Years of Human Sexual Culture*. Bantam, 1996: 282.

Legal Highs. Erowid website. [www.erowid.org]. § Lycaeum website. [www.lycaeum.org].

DEA Ruling. Randall, R.C. (editor). *Marijuana, Medicine and the Law*, Volumes I and II. Galen Press, 1988 and 1989. The two volumes present testimony and documents from the DEA's hearings.

Drug Warnings. US Food and Drug Administration. "Safety-Related Drug Labeling Changes" on the page "Medical Product Safety Information." FDA website [www.fda.gov]

SUVs. Bureau of Transportation Statistics, US Department of Transportation. "National Transportation Statistics 2003." March 2004 [www.bts.gov]. § Harborview Injury Prevention and Research Center at the University of Washington. "Light Trucks Pose Greater Injury Risk to Pedestrians" [press release]. 15 June 2004.

Aristotle. Asimov, Isaac. *Isaac Asimov's Book of Facts*. Fawcett Columbine Books, 1979. § Kaisler, Denise. "Comet Misconceptions." Undated paper on doctoral student Kaisler's site on the website of UCLA's Division of Astronomy and Astrophysics [www.astro.ucla.edu/~kaisler/]. § Wilson, Prof. Fred L. "Science and Human Values: Aristotle." Undated paper on Dr. Wilson's site on the Rochester Institute of Technology website [www.rit.edu/~flwstv/]. § "Aristotle." "Atom." "Democritus." *Encyclopedia Britannica*.

Native American Slaves. Bailey, L.R. *Indian Slave Trade in the Southwest*. Tower Publications, 1966. § Gallay, Alan. *The Indian Slave Trade: The Rise of the English Empire in the American South, 1960-1717*. Yale University Press, 2002. § Perdue, Theda. "Slavery." Entry in *Encyclopedia of North American Indians*. Frederick E. Hoxie, ed. Houghton Mifflin Company, 1996.

Washington's Graft. A Calm Observer. "A Calm Observer." In *Shaking the Foundations: 200 Years of Investigative Journalism in America*. Bruce Shapiro, ed. Thunder's Mouth Press and Nation Books, 2003.

Declaration Slur. Texts of the US Declaration of Independence and the original California Constitution of 1879. § Manheim, Prof. Karl. "Discrimination against Chinese in California." Undated paper on Dr. Manheim's site on the Loyola Law School website [class.lls.edu/~manheimk].

Audubon. Hart-Davis, Duff. *Audubon's Elephant: America's Greatest Naturalist and the Making of* The Birds of America. Henry Holt and Company, 2004. § May, Stephen. "John James Audubon: Squire of Mill Grove and Genius of Art and Science." *Pennsylvania Heritage Magazine*. Reprinted on jjaudubon.com. § "John James Audubon." *Encyclopædia Britannica*. 2004. § "John James Audubon 1785-1851." National Audubon Society website [www.audubon.org].

Lynchings. Carrigan, William D. "The Lynching of Persons of Mexican Origin or Descent in the United States, 1848 to 1928." *Journal of Social History*, Winter 2003. § Zangrando, Robert L. "About Lynching." *The Reader's Companion to American History*. Eric Foner and John A. Garraty, eds. Houghton Mifflin, 1991. § "Georgia Lynching Victims." *Atlanta-Journal Constitution* website [www.ajc.com], 16 May 2002. § "Lynching." The Handbook of Texas Online [www.tsha.utexas.edu].

Freud. Crews, Frederick, ed. *Unauthorized Freud: Doubters Confront a Legend*. Penguin Books, 1999. Especially the following chapters: "Anna O.: The First Tall Tale" by Mikkel Borch-Jacobsen; "Delusions and Dream in Freud's 'Dora'" by Allen Esterson; "Exemplary Botches" by Frank J. Sulloway; "A Little Child Shall Mislead Them" by Joseph Wolpe and Stanley Rachman; Crews' "Overview" of Part III.

Monopoly. Anspach, Ralph. *The Billion Dollar Monopoly Swindle: The True Story Behind Monopoly*. Self-published, 1998. § Anti-Monopoly website [www.antimonopoly.com]. § Monopoly website [www.hasbro.com/monopoly/].

Gandhi. Chadha, Yogesh. *Gandhi: A Life*. John Wiley & Sons, 1997: 395-7. § Payne, Robert. *The Life and Death of Mahatma Gandhi*. Smithmark Publishers, 1995: 501-6. § Both of these books, although sympathetic to Gandhi overall, cover many of his warts. For a no-hold-barred look at his hypocrisies, see *Gandhi: Behind the Mask of Divinity*.

Americans in Concentration Camps. Bard, Mitchell G. *Forgotten Victims: The Abandonment of Americans in Hitler's Camps*. Westview Press, 1994.

Nuke Accidents. CNN. "US Nuclear Bomb 'on Seabed off Greenland'." CNN website, 13 Aug 2000. § Environment, Safety and Health, US Department of Energy. "Palomares, Spain Medical Surveillance and Environmental Monitoring Program." [tis.eh.doe.gov/health/]. § Tiwari, Jaya, and Clovo J. Gray. "US Nuclear Weapons Accidents." Center for Defense Information website [www.cdi.org]. § United Press International. "Nuclear Near-Disaster Reportedly Covered Up." *Sun-News*, 11 June 1979. § US Nuclear Weapons Cost Study Project, Foreign Policy Studies Program. "The Palomares "Broken Arrow," January 1966" Brookings Institution [www.brook.edu] § "List of Nuclear Accidents." Wikipedia [wikipedia.org]. § "Nuclear Accidents" section on Nuclearfiles.org.

Missile Code. Blair, Bruce G. "Keeping Presidents in the Nuclear Dark (Episode #1: The Case of the Missing 'Permissive Action Links')." Center for Defense Intelligence website [www.cdi.org], 11 Feb 2004.

REFERENCES

Land Giveaway. Environmental Working Group. "Who Owns the West?" [report]. 2004. [www.ewg.org/mining].

Corporate Tax Evasion. General Accounting Office. "Comparison of the Reported Tax Liabilities of Foreign- and U.S.-Controlled Corporations, 1996-2000." Feb 2004. GAO-04-358. § McKinnon, John D. "Many Companies Avoided Taxes Even as Profits Soared in Boom." *Wall Street Journal*, 06 April 2004: A1.

Discharge Codes. Associated Press. "Pentagon Abolishes Code on Discharges of Military Misfits." *New York Times*, 23 Mar 1974. § Kihss, Peter. "Use of Personal-Characterization Coding on Military Discharges Is Assailed." *New York Times*, 30 Sep 1973. § The American War Library website [members.aol.com/veterans/]. This site used to list the meanings for hundreds of SPN codes, but at some point it removed this information.

Homeless Vets. Stewart, Jocelyn Y. "From the Ranks to the Street." *Los Angeles Times*, 29 May 2004. § National Coalition for Homeless Veterans website [www.nchv.org]. § US Department of Veterans Affairs website [www.va.gov].

Prison Population. Bureau of Justice Statistics, Office of Justice Programs, US Department of Justice. [www.ojp.usdoj.gov/bjs/]. § Research Development and Statistics Directorate, UK Home Office. "World Prison Population List" (fourth edition), 2003. [www.homeoffice.gov.uk/rds/]. § November Coalition website [www.november.org].

Asset Forfeiture. Fishburn, Mike. "Gored by the Ox: A Discussion of the Federal and Texas Laws That Empower Civil-Asset Forfeiture." *Rutgers Law Record*, 26.4 (2002). § Asset Forfeiture Program, Department of Justice website [www.usdoj.gov/jmd/afp/]. § Executive Office for Asset Forfeiture, Department of Treasury website [www.treas.gov/offices/eotffc/teoaf/]. § Forfeiture Endangers American Rights website [www.fear.org]

EPA. Jenkins, Cate, PhD. "Comments on the EPA Office of Inspector General's 1/27/03 Interim Report Titled: 'EPA's Response to the World Trade Center Towers Collapse.'" Environmental Protection Agency, 04 July 2003. § Office of Inspector General, US Environmental Protection Agency. "EPA's Response to the World Trade Center

Collapse: Challenges, Successes and Areas for Improvement." 21 Aug 2003. Report #2003-P-00012. § Smith, Sam. "9/11 Memo Reveals Asbestos 'Cover-up'." *New York Post*, 16 July 2004. § Press releases on the EPA website [www.epa.gov].

Condoleezza Rice. Central Intelligence Agency. "Bin Ladin Determined to Strike In US." President Daily Brief, 6 Aug 2001. Released 10 Aug 2004. Widely published in the media. § Transcript of Rice's testimony before the National Commission on Terrorist Attacks Upon the United States, 8 April 2004. Published on the websites of CNN and NYT, among others.

Al Qaeda. Congressional Research Service. "Terrorist Attacks by al Qaeda." 31 March 2004. Posted on the House Committee on Government Reform Minority Office website [www.house.gov/reform/min/].

Patriot Act. Lichtblau, Eric. "US Cautiously Begins to Seize Millions in Foreign Banks." *New York Times*, 30 May 2003. § Lichtblau, Eric. "Patriot Act Goes Beyond Terror." *New York Times*, 28 Sept 2003. § Murphy, Kevin. "8-Year Sentence for Radio Interference, UW Grad's Actions Labeled Terrorism." *Capital Times* (Madison, WI), 13 May 2004. § Unsigned. "Hauling Cash Lands Man In Jail." AlaNews Network, 23 Dec 2003. § US Department of Justice. "Report from the Field: The USA PATRIOT Act at Work." July 2004. § Preserving Life and Liberty website [www.lifeandliberty.gov].

Iraq Reasons. Cooper, Richard T. "General Casts War in Religious Terms." *Los Angeles Times*, 16 Oct 2003. § Unsigned. "US Expert Slams WMD 'Delusions'." BBC, 5 June 2004. § Transcript of *Meet the Press* [TV show], 14 Sept 2003. § Largio, Devon M. "Uncovering the Rationales for the War on Iraq: The Words of the Bush Administration, Congress, and the Media from September 12, 2001 to October 11, 2002." Thesis for the Degree of Bachelor of Arts in Political Science, College of Liberal Arts and Sciences, University of Illinois, Urbana-Champaign, Illinois. 2004. § King, John. "Bush Calls Saddam 'the Guy Who Tried to Kill My Dad'." CNN, 27 Sept 2002. § Mekay, Emad. "Iraq War Launched to Protect Israel - Bush Adviser." Inter Press Service, 29 Mar 2004. § "Deputy Secretary Wolfowitz Interview with Sam Tannenhaus, *Vanity Fair*" [transcript]. Department of Defense website, 09 May 2003 [www.dod.gov]. § "Quotation of the

Day." *New York Times*, 07 Sept 2002: A6. § *Congressional Record — House*, 15 June 2004: H4117, H4120. § Harnden, Toby. "Ousting Saddam 'Would be Good Business'." *Daily Telegraph* (London), 17 Sept 2002. § Moran, Michael, and Alex Johnson. "Oil After Saddam: All Bets Are in." MSNBC, 7 Nov 2002. § Schweizer, Peter, and Rochelle Schweizer. *The Bushes: Portrait of a Dynasty*. Doubleday, 2004.

Illegal War. Burkeman, Oliver, and Julian Borger. "War Critics Astonished as US Hawk Admits Invasion Was Illegal." *Guardian* (London). 20 Nov 2003. § Perle's biography on the American Enterprise Institute website [www.aei.org].

Secret Prisons. Human Rights First. "Ending Secret Detentions" [report]. June 2004. § Aldinger, Charles. "Halliburton to Build New Cells at Guantanamo Base." Reuters, 27 July 2002. § Bartelme, Tony. "The Navy's Secret Brig." *Post and Courier* (Charleston, SC), 23 Nov 2003.

Child Porn Database. General Accounting Office. "File-Sharing Programs: Users of Peer-to-Peer Networks Can Readily Access Child Pornography. Statement of Linda D. Koontz, Director, Information Management Issues." 09 Sept 2003. GAO-03-1115T. § Department of Homeland Security. "Fact Sheet: Operation Predator." 09 July 2003.

Presidential Debates. Open Debates website [www.opendebates.org].

Water Dumping. Office of Compliance, Office of Enforcement and Compliance Assurance, US Environmental Protection Agency. "Profile of the Ground Transportation Industry: Trucking, Railroad, and Pipeline." Sept 1997. EPA/310-R-97-002. § Office of Enforcement and Compliance Assurance, US Environmental Protection Agency. "Enforcement and Compliance Assurance Accomplishments Report FY 1997." July 1998. EPA-300-R-98-003. § US Code, Title 33, Chapter 9, Subchapter 1, Sections 407 & 411.

Drugs in Water. Kolpin, DW, *et al*. "Pharmaceuticals, Hormones, and Other Organic Wastewater Contaminants in US Streams, 1999-2000: A National Reconnaissance." *Environmental Science and Technology* 36.6 (2002): 1202-11. § Morson, Berny. "Test Finds Boulder Creek Is Potpourri of Chemicals." *Rocky Mountain News* (Denver, CO), 29 Oct 2003.

§ National Ground Water Association. "Proceedings of the 2nd International Conference on Pharmaceuticals and Endocrine Disrupting Chemicals in Water, October 9-11, 2001, Minneapolis, Minnesota." NGWA, undated. § Stiles, Nikki. "The Mystery Behind PPCPs." *Small Flows Quarterly* 5.1 (winter 2004). § US Environmental Protection Agency. Pharmaceuticals and Personal Care Products (PPCPs) as Environmental Pollutants website [www.epa.gov/nerlesd1/chemistry/pharma/].

Chemical Weapons. Defence Publishing Service, Department of Defence (Australia). "Chemical Warfare Agent Sea Dumping off Australia" (revised and updated edition). 2003. § Hogendoorn, E.J. "A Chemical Weapons Atlas." *Bulletin of the Atomic Scientists* 53.5 (Sept/Oct 1997). § Simons, Marlise. "Discarded War Munitions Leach Poisons Into the Baltic." *New York Times*, 20 June 2003.

Cigarette Butts. Unsigned. "Cigarette Butts Cause Environmental Pollution." Reuters, 24 May 1999. § Anne Landman's Collection at Tobacco Documents Online [tobaccodocuments.org/landman/]. § BUTTsOUT website [www.buttsout.net]. § Cigarette Litter website. [www.cigarettelitter.org]. § Smart Ashtray website [www.smartashtray.com].

Caviar. Cooper, Simon. "Caviar." *SEED Magazine*, Nov 2003: 93-101, 125-9.

Hippocratic Oath. Website of the *NOVA* episode "Survivor M.D.," from the Public Broadcasting System, March-April 2001. [www.pbs.org/wgbh/nova/doctors/]. The original oath quoted is the 1943 English-language translation by Ludwig Edelstein.

Hysterectomies. Bouchez, Colette. "Hysterectomy: The Operation Women May Not Need." ABCNews.com, 11 Dec 2002. § Broder, Michael S., MD, *et al.* "The Appropriateness of Recommendations for Hysterectomy" [abstract]. *Obstetrics & Gynecology* 2000;95:199-205. § West, Stanley, MD, with Paula Dranov. *The Hysterectomy Hoax: The Truth About Why Many Hysterectomies Are Unnecessary and How to Avoid Them* (third edition). Next Decade, Inc., 2002.

Human Experimentation. Barnett, Antony. "UK Firm Tried HIV Drug on Orphans." *Observer* (London). 4 April 2004. § Basu, Indrajit. "India's Clinical Trials and Tribulations." *Asia Times*, 23 July 2004. § Hyder, A.A., *et al.* "Ethical Review of Health Research: A Perspective From Developing Country Researchers" [abstract]. *Journal of Medical Ethics* 2004;30:68-72. § Johns Hopkins University Bloomberg School of Public Health. "Ethical Review of Research in Developing Countries Needed" [press release], 24 Feb 2004. § Scheff, Liam. "The House That AIDS Built." AltHeal website [www.altheal.org], Jan 2004.

Sunscreen. Cedric F. Garland. "More on Preventing Skin Cancer." *British Medical Journal*, 2003;327:1228 (22 November). § Thompson, Larry. "Sunscreen, Skin Cancer, and UVA." HealthLink (Medical College of Wisconsin), 26 July 2000. [healthlink.mcw.edu]. § Mercola.com, website of Dr. Joseph Mercola.

Head Transplants. Bennun, David. "Dr. Robert White." *Sunday Telegraph Magazine* (London), 2000. Reprinted at the author's website [bennun.biz]. § Roach, Mary. *Stiff: The Curious Lives of Human Cadavers.* Norton, 2003. § **Sidebar**: ShuffleBrain, the website of Paul Pietsch, PhD [www.indiana.edu/~pietsch].

Spanish Flu. Billings, Molly. "The Influenza Pandemic of 1918." Human Virology website, Stanford University [www.stanford.edu/group/virus/]. § Davies, Pete. *Devil's Flu: The World's Deadliest Influenza Epidemic and the Scientific Hunt for the Virus That Caused It.* Owl Books, 2000. § *MacNeil/Lehrer NewsHour.* "Revisiting the 1918 Flu" [interview]. Public Broadcasting System, 24 Mar 1997. § Office of the Inspector General, US Department of Agriculture. "Controls Over Biological, Chemical, and Radioactive Materials at Institutions Funded by the US Department of Agriculture" [audit report]. Sept 2003. 50099-14-At. § The Sunshine Project. "Recreating the Spanish Flu?" [briefing paper]. 9 Oct 2003. [www.sunshine-project.org].

Pedo-Priest Cover-up. The Supreme and Holy Congregation of the Holy Office. "Instruction on the Manner of Proceeding in Cases of Solicitation." The Vatican Press, 1962. § Barnett, Antony. "Vatican Ordered Bishops Worldwide to Cover up Priests' Sex Abuses." *Observer* (London), 17 Aug 2003. § Unsigned. "Sex Policy Order a 'Smoking Gun'

Pointing at Vatican." Reuters, 12 Dec 2002. § Sullivan, Jack. "Medeiros, Vatican Involved in Coverup." *Boston Herald*, 16 May 2002.

God's Name. Various translations of the Bible. § *A Concise Dictionary of the Words in the Hebrew Bible* by James Strongs. Online at Blue Letter Bible [blueletterbible.org].